Contents

At the pond

Find a pond.

Look around!

What lives here?

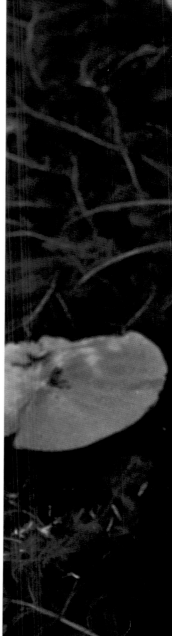

What's in a Pond?

by Martha E. H. Rustad

raintree
a Capstone company — publishers for children

Raintree is an imprint of Capstone Global Library Limited, a company incorporated in England and Wales having its registered office at 7 Pilgrim Street, London, EC4V 6LB – Registered company number: 6695582

www.raintree.co.uk
myorders@raintree.co.uk

Text © Capstone Global Library Limited 2016
The moral rights of the proprietor have been asserted.

Edited by Erika L. Shores
Designed by Cynthia Della-Rovere
Picture research by Svetlana Zhurkin
Production by Katy LaVigne

ISBN 978 1 4747 0604 9
19 18 17 16 15
10 9 8 7 6 5 4 3 2 1

British Library Cataloguing in Publication Data
A full catalogue record for this book is available from the British Library.

Acknowledgements
Alamy: Marvin Dembinsky Photo Associates, 5; iStockphoto: Michelinedesgroseilliers, 17; Newscom: Photoshot/NHPA/Stephen Krasemann, 21; Shutterstock: CCat82, 9 (back), Dan Mensinger, 7 (inset), Dirk Ercken, 3, Eric Isselee, back cover, 8, Ian Grainger, 10, Iliuta Goean, 13, Josef Bosak, 15, Karen Hermann, 7 (back), MyImages Micha, 11, panbazil, 4, perlphoto, 9 (inset), rolfik, 1, 14, Tea Maeklong, 6, 12, 20, Vetapi, 18—19, Yuriy Kulik, cover

Every effort has been made to contact copyright holders of material reproduced in this book. Any omissions will be rectified in subsequent printings if notice is given to the publisher.

All the internet addresses (URLs) given in this book were valid at the time of going to press. However, due to the dynamic nature of the internet, some addresses may have changed, or sites may have changed or ceased to exist since publication. While the author and publisher regret any inconvenience this may cause readers, no responsibility for any such changes can be accepted by either the author or the publisher.

Printed in China.

Pond plants

Look!

Tiny algae float in ponds.

They make rocks slippery.

algae

Reeds grow tall.

Lily pads float.

reeds

lily pad

Pond animals

Tadpoles swim.

They grow into frogs.

tadpoles

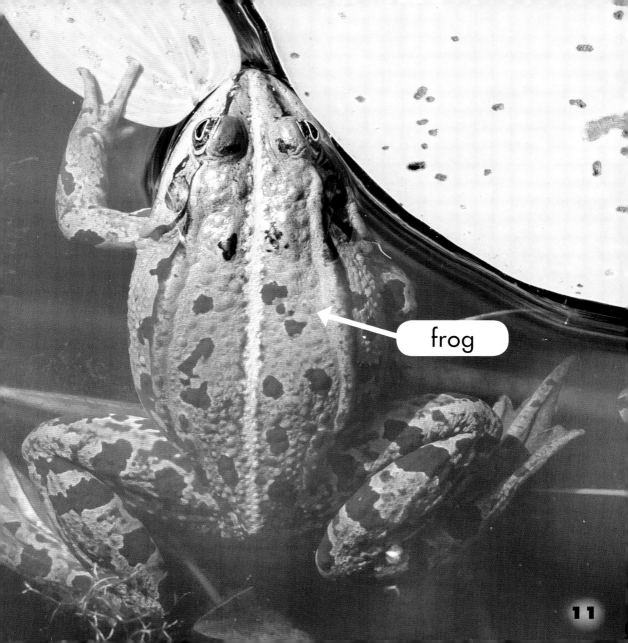

frog

Dragonflies fly low.

They eat flying insects.

Snap!

A turtle catches a fish.

Shy turtles hide.

Swish!

Tiny minnows dart.

They lay eggs at

the bottom of the pond.

Quack!

Baby ducks follow mum.

She teaches them to swim.

A beaver cuts down a tree.

He builds a dam.

It makes a pond.

Ponds make good homes.

Glossary

algae tiny floating plants

dam barrier built in a stream by a beaver

minnow small fish

reed tall, thin plant that grows in wetlands, marshes and ponds

tadpole young frog at a stage when it has an oval head and long tail, and lives in water

Read more

Life Story of a Frog (Animal Life Stories), Charlotte Guillain (Raintree, 2014)

Pond (Look Inside a…), Richard and Louise Spilsbury (Raintree, 2013)

Ponds (Water, Water, Everywhere!) Diyan Leake (Raintree, 2014)

Websites

www.bbc.co.uk/nature/habitats/Lake
Find out more about lakes and ponds.

www.bbc.co.uk/nature/life/Common_frog
Learn all about frogs.

Index

lonely planet KIDS

ATLAS
of
DOGS

illustrated by
Kelsey Heaton

written by
Frances Evans

CONTENTS

A WORLD OF DOGS

Welcome to the wonderful world of dogs! From the Alaskan Malamute to the Weimaraner and the Afghan hound to the Yorkshire terrier, dogs hold an incredibly special place in hearts and homes all over the globe. This book will take you on a woof-tastic journey across the continents and introduce you to more than 130 brilliant breeds and crossbreeds. Some are pooches you might bump into at the park, while others will be less familiar fluffsters.

It's estimated that there are 900 million dogs in the world.

HOW THIS BOOK WORKS

You'll find a map at the start of each chapter so you can see where the dogs come from, while profile pages give you the lowdown on each breed, their background and care needs. There are also special entries that explore breed groups, heroic hounds, cuddly puppies, doggie dancing and much more!

WHAT IS A DOG?

Dogs are so much more than a wet nose and a waggy tail – they are our oldest and most constant animal friends. All dogs are descended from ancient wolves, which were the first animals to be tamed (or 'domesticated') by humans at least 14,000 years ago. Dogs have stood faithfully by our side ever since, helping us to hunt and herd, protecting us from danger, assisting people in need and, above all, offering comfort and companionship. They are truly remarkable animals.

WHAT IS A BREED?

From titchy Chihuahuas to giant Great Danes, dogs come in an amazing range of shapes and sizes. Over thousands of years, people have deliberately bred different dogs so they have particular qualities. These qualities might be practical skills, such as a talent for herding sheep, behavioural traits, like friendliness, or physical features – floppy ears or curly hair, for example. This process is called 'selective breeding'.

A group of dogs that has been bred to have the same characteristics and features is known as a 'breed'. Different breeds have developed over time in different parts of the world, and they often reflect the environment they come from. The speedy sloughi (1) was built to race across the Sahara desert, the hefty St Bernard (2) was made to climb up mountains in the Swiss Alps, and the elegant shih tzu (3) was bred for a life of luxury inside Chinese palaces. You can think of all the breeds you meet in this book as doggie ambassadors for their home nations and cultures.

A 'breed' isn't a scientific term. It is just a way that groups of dog breeders, known as kennel clubs, identify different types of dogs. This means that what makes a breed – and whether a type of dog is considered a breed at all – can vary in different countries of the world and between different kennel clubs.

OWNING A DOG

Owning a dog is a great privilege, but it is also a big responsibility. If you're thinking of welcoming a furry friend into your family, it's important to research breeds and to think carefully about how your lifestyle will suit different dogs. This book will give you an introduction to the characters and care needs of various different breeds and crossbreeds.

The best way to get a dog is by adopting through a rescue or rehoming centre, where all sorts of dogs are looked after until they are matched with loving homes. If you decide to buy a puppy, make sure you use a reputable breeder, who will be an expert on the breed and take good care of their dogs. Never buy a dog online or a puppy without seeing it with its mum in a happy home environment.

ATLAS OF A DOG

Whether they're short and sturdy like the Pekingese or tall and slender like the borzoi, all dogs share the same essential features. Here's some basic dog geography.

HEAD SHAPES

Dogs' heads come in three basic shapes: a medium-sized head with a medium-length muzzle (such as a Labrador, p14), a wide head with a short muzzle (such as a bulldog, p41) and a long thin head (such as a greyhound, p41).

EAR SHAPES

The exact shape and size of ears varies between breeds, but they are normally pointed, folded or droopy. This variety is the result of humans breeding dogs to have particular features. Originally, all dogs would have had pointed ears like wolves.

MUZZLE

A dog's snout is often called a 'muzzle'. Some breeds have longer or shorter muzzles than others.

TONGUE

A dog uses its tongue to taste, clean itself and communicate – if you get a lick from a dog, you know it really likes you! Dogs also rely on their tongues to keep them cool, as they aren't able to sweat like humans. If a dog feels hot, it will pant to cool itself down.

TEETH

An adult dog has 42 teeth in total. The four fang-like teeth at the front of a dog's mouth are called 'canines' and they're used to tear up food. The smaller teeth at the front are for gripping and the back teeth grind down tougher snacks.

A dog's height is measured from the tip of its toes to the top of its shoulder (rather than the top of its head). In this book, each breed's size – small, medium, large or giant – is listed in its profile box.

COAT

Many dogs have a 'double coat' made up of a soft under layer to keep warm and a rougher outer layer that's weatherproof. But some breeds only have a single coat and some don't have any hair at all! The length and colour of a dog's coat varies greatly between breeds.

TAIL

A dog uses its tail to express how it's feeling, and for balance when walking or running. While most dogs have long tails, some breeds are born with naturally short or stumpy waggers.

PAWS

A dog has a paw pad for each of its toes. These pads act as shock absorbers, protecting the dog's feet when they are walking or running, as well as providing insulation.

CLAWS

Most dogs have four nails on each of their back feet and five on each of their front feet. The extra nails on the front paws are called 'dewclaws'. Some dogs use their dewclaws to give them extra grip when they run or when they hold on to a chew.

SUPER SENSES

Like humans, dogs rely on their senses – smell, sight, hearing, taste and touch. But the way dogs use these senses is quite different to us.

HEARING

The way a dog hears is very different from a human. Dogs can hear high-pitched sounds and soft, faraway sounds that we can't detect. Some studies have even suggested that dogs might be able to pick up the high-pitched noises deep underground that happen before an earthquake or tsunami (see page 95).

To greet a dog, offer it your hand so it can approach you to have a gentle sniff. This is a dog's way of saying hello and getting to know you. Never force your hand in a dog's face – if it's happy to say hi, it will come up to you.

SMELL

A dog's top sense is smell. Dogs rely on their sense of smell to get information about their world and to communicate. Just think of how dogs say 'hello' to each other! The average pooch has around 100 million scent receptors in its nose, compared to a human's puny 5 million. This means dogs can detect smells we aren't aware of. They can also break down complex information contained in a scent. For example, while you'd smell the tasty, cheesy 'pizza-ness' of a freshly cooked pizza, a dog would smell every individual ingredient – the cheese, the tomato, the dough, and each herb and spice that went into the sauce.

It's important to allow a dog time to stop and sniff things when out on a walk. Having a good sniff of a patch of grass or a lamp post gives a dog essential information about what's going on around it and exercises its brain.

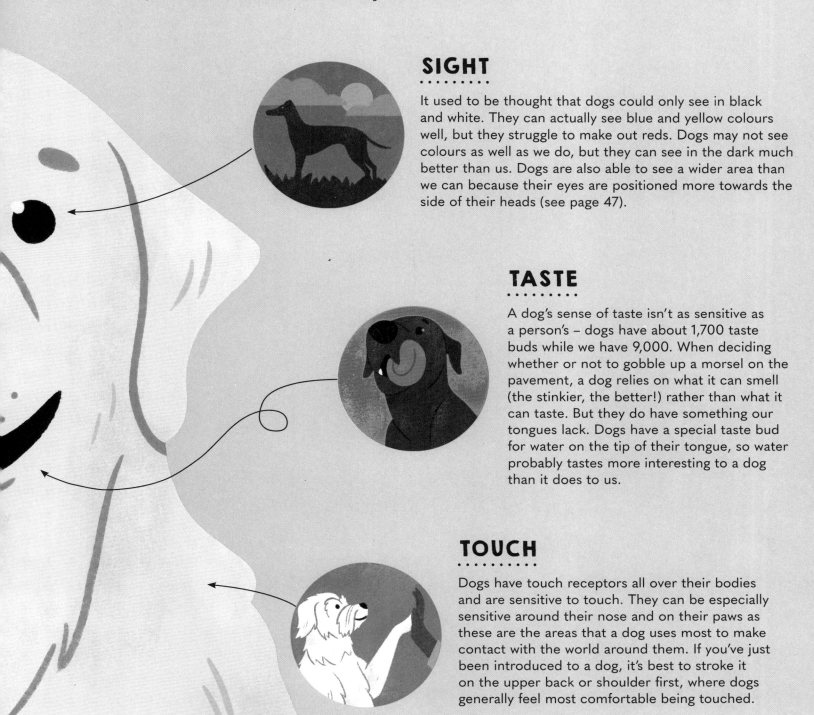

When a dog kicks the ground after going to the loo, it's not trying to cover its poop up. Dogs have scent glands on their paws and they use their smelly feet to say 'hello' to other dogs. By scratching the ground, they are transferring their special smell so other canines know they've been there.

SIGHT

It used to be thought that dogs could only see in black and white. They can actually see blue and yellow colours well, but they struggle to make out reds. Dogs may not see colours as well as we do, but they can see in the dark much better than us. Dogs are also able to see a wider area than we can because their eyes are positioned more towards the side of their heads (see page 47).

TASTE

A dog's sense of taste isn't as sensitive as a person's – dogs have about 1,700 taste buds while we have 9,000. When deciding whether or not to gobble up a morsel on the pavement, a dog relies on what it can smell (the stinkier, the better!) rather than what it can taste. But they do have something our tongues lack. Dogs have a special taste bud for water on the tip of their tongue, so water probably tastes more interesting to a dog than it does to us.

TOUCH

Dogs have touch receptors all over their bodies and are sensitive to touch. They can be especially sensitive around their nose and on their paws as these are the areas that a dog uses most to make contact with the world around them. If you've just been introduced to a dog, it's best to stroke it on the upper back or shoulder first, where dogs generally feel most comfortable being touched.

GREENLAND DOG
GREENLAND

NEWFOUNDLAND
CANADA

BOSTON TERRIER
USA

CHINOOK
USA

NOVA SCOTIA DUCK-TOLLING RETRIEVER
CANADA

An Alaskan Malamute was the inspiration behind Chewbacca in the Star Wars films. The films' creator, George Lucas, had a pet Malamute called Indiana who sat by his side while he wrote the script.

ALASKAN MALAMUTE
USA

LABRADOR RETRIEVER
CANADA

AMERICAN WATER SPANIEL
USA

AMERICAN COCKER SPANIEL
USA

NORTH AMERICA

From the super-floofy to the fur-free, North America is home to an incredible mix of dogs. Many North American breeds were developed with a particular job in mind – whether that's pulling a sledge through a snowstorm, rounding up cattle on the prairie or guarding homes in the Wild West. Others are more at home trotting through city parks or strutting their stuff in a show ring. Let's meet them!

A Boston terrier crossbreed called Sergeant Stubby fought in 17 battles during World War I. This heroic hound helped find wounded soldiers and warned his regiment of attacks.

CHESAPEAKE BAY RETRIEVER
USA

HAVANESE
CUBA

MOUNTAIN CUR
USA

AMERICAN BULLDOG
USA

XOLOITZCUINTLI
MEXICO

A loyal (and very greedy) Xoloitzcuintli called Dante appears in the Disney/Pixar film Coco.

AUSTRALIAN SHEPHERD
USA

BLACK-AND-TAN COONHOUND
USA

CHIHUAHUA MEXICO

The smallest dog in the world by height was a Chihuahua called Milly. She was just 9.65 cm (3.8 in) from her foot to her shoulder, meaning she was smaller than a can of cola!

LABRADOR RETRIEVER

With webbed feet, an otter-like tail and weatherproof fur, these gentle dogs are built for swimming. They originally came from Newfoundland in Canada, where they were trained to fetch fishermen's nets from the sea. Today's Labradors still love being around water and will happily spend hours bounding in and out of a river after a tennis ball.

POOCH PROFILE:

Country: Canada **Size:** Large; 55–57 cm (22 in) tall **Coat:** Short fur; black, yellow or chocolate **Personality:** Loving, friendly, clever

Kind expression

Thick tail, which the dog uses to steer when swimming

Dense topcoat to repel water

Soft mouth

Strong legs

Round paws with webbed feet

Soft undercoat to keep the dog warm

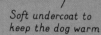

Labradors are smart, eager-to-please dogs and make excellent family pets, assistance dogs and guide dogs. As well as being immensely loyal, Labs are also immensely greedy, so you need to keep an eye on how many treats you're giving them – they will always have room for more!

NEWFOUNDLAND

No, it's not a cuddly bear, it's a Newfoundland! These sweet-natured giants get their name from an area of north-eastern Canada where they were originally used as the ultimate fisherman's friend. With big, powerful bodies, their jobs ranged from pulling carts of fish to jumping off boats to bring back nets or lost equipment.

The breed's swimming skills and love of people make Newfoundlands the perfect water-rescue dogs. If you ever go swimming with a Newfie, they will almost certainly try to pull you back to dry land.

These dogs have loose lips so they drool a lot – always keep a towel handy!

Thick, double-layered coat

Oily, waterproof fur

Strong body

Webbed feet for swimming

POOCH PROFILE:
Country: Canada **Size:** Giant; 66–71 cm (26–28 in) tall **Coat:** Dense, medium-length fur; black, grey, brown or white with black markings
Personality: Happy, loyal, gentle

Bright, gentle expression

Constantly moving tail

Compact body

Webbed feet

NOVA SCOTIA DUCK-TOLLING RETRIEVER

This small retriever was first bred by huntsmen in Nova Scotia in the 1800s to help them find and collect ducks. The wavy movement of the dog's tail is said to distract ducks, allowing people to catch them. In fact, the 'tolling' part of the dog's name comes from an old word that means 'to entice'.

Tollers are pretty dogs, with feathery, copper-coloured fur. They like to be on the go and have busy brains, which makes them perfect for activities such as agility training.

POOCH PROFILE:
Country: Canada **Size:** Medium; 43–53 cm (17–21 in) tall **Coat:** Medium-length fur; red or orange colour with white markings **Personality:** Playful, outgoing, smart

GREENLAND DOG

With thick bones and even thicker fur, these powerful dogs are made for life in a tough, cold climate. They are the only breed to come from Greenland, an island close to the North Pole, where they've been used for centuries to pull heavy sledges across the snow.

Their sledging skills have also taken Greenland dogs to the other end of the world. The Norwegian explorer Roald Amundsen used teams of Greenland dogs in his expedition to Antarctica between 1910 and 1912, and it was partly thanks to the strength and stamina of the dogs that Amundsen became the first person to reach the South Pole.

POOCH PROFILE:
Country: Greenland **Size:** Large; 51–68 cm (20–27 in) tall **Coat:** Thick, double coat; comes in all colours **Personality:** Bold, good-natured, dignified

Large, bushy tail

Very thick double-layered coat

Short ears, protected from the cold by dense fur

Undercoat can be up to 5 cm (2 in) long

Thick paw pads with strong nails

ALASKAN MALAMUTE

Some of the oldest Arctic sled dogs, Malamutes are thought to be descended from the wolf-dogs that travelled with humans into North America over 4,000 years ago. Named after the Inuit Mahlemut tribe, these dogs were bred to pull heavy loads over long distances and in freezing conditions.

Malamutes may look tough, but they like to be part of the pack and will want to be involved in whatever you're up to. (If you leave them out, be warned – they will howl!) They need plenty of exercise and attention to keep them happy, and daily brushing to keep that fluffy coat looking its best.

Fur inside ears and between toes to keep in as much heat as possible

Not a noisy breed, but has a characteristic 'woo woo' howl

Dense fur that's particularly thick around the neck

Powerful shoulders

Loosely curled tail

Thick paw pads for running on ice and snow

POOCH PROFILE:
Country: USA **Size:** Large; 58–64 cm (23–25 in) tall **Coat:** Thick, double coat; grey, black or red with white markings; can also be all white **Personality:** Intelligent, affectionate, sociable

CHESAPEAKE BAY RETRIEVER

It's thought that American huntsmen bred Newfoundlands with retrievers and hounds to create the 'Chessie'. Everything about the breed is custom-built for the environment of Chesapeake Bay, a 320-km (200-mile) long estuary on America's east coast. Chessies have thick, oily coats to protect them in the freezing-cold sea and muscular bodies for swimming through choppy waters to collect ducks.

Although they look like woolly-coated Labradors (p12), Chessies are more independent dogs. They'll bond strongly with their human family but can be aloof with strangers and need to be kept active and busy. The life of a happy Chessie is full of long walks and LOTS of swimming.

POOCH PROFILE:
Country: USA **Size:** Large; 53–66 cm (21–26 in) tall **Coat:** Unusual wavy fur; colours from light to deep brown and red **Personality:** Affectionate, sensitive, hard-working

Short, thick coat with a wavy texture

Straight or slightly curved tail, used like a rudder when swimming

Deep chest for cutting through the water

Strong, muscly body

Fur repels water

Large, webbed feet

CHINOOK

The official dog of the state of New Hampshire in the USA, the chinook was created by Arthur Walden, a local adventurer. Walden returned home from an Alaskan expedition determined to breed his own sled dogs. It's said he crossed a mastiff-type dog with a Greenland dog to make the chinook (an Inuit word meaning 'warm wind').

After Walden died, the breed nearly went extinct and in the 1960s, the *Guinness Book of World Records* named it the rarest breed in the world. Since then, chinooks have been brought back from the brink. Kind-natured and easy to train, they make great family pets and are very gentle with kids.

Intelligent, kind expression

Usually have darker fur around the nose and eyes

Feathery tail

Floppy ears

Muscly, strong body

POOCH PROFILE:
Country: USA **Size:** Large; 55–66 cm (22–26 in) tall **Coat:** Medium-length, smooth coat; tawny-coloured **Personality:** Friendly, patient, clever

BOSTON TERRIER

With sparkly eyes, a stylish coat and a friendly nature, it's easy to see why the Boston terrier is nicknamed the 'American gentleman'. These dapper little dogs were first developed in the 19th century by crossing a British bulldog (p41) with a now-extinct breed called a white English terrier. They've been a firm favourite in American households ever since.

Named after the capital city of the state of Massachusetts, Boston terriers are true town dwellers. They're compact and easy-going, and just as happy lounging with you on the sofa as they are trotting round the park. Although Bostons need walks, their flat noses mean they can't breathe as easily as longer-snouted dogs, so they shouldn't be over exercised, particularly in hot weather.

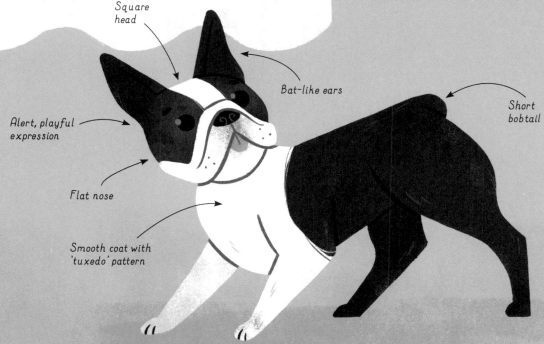

Square head

Bat-like ears

Short bobtail

Alert, playful expression

Flat nose

Smooth coat with 'tuxedo' pattern

POOCH PROFILE:
Country: USA **Size:** Small–Medium; 38–43 cm (15–17 in) tall **Coat:** Short and shiny; black or brindle with white markings **Personality:** Cheerful, smart, strong-minded

Boston terriers are the smallest type of bulldog and they look quite different from their European cousins. While British bulldogs have large, wrinkly heads and stocky bodies, Boston terriers are slimmer, with small heads and naturally pointy ears.

AMERICAN COCKER SPANIEL

With long, glossy coats and dreamy eyes, American cocker spaniels are the Hollywood stars of the dog world. Quite literally – the pampered pooch in Disney's *Lady and the Tramp* is an American cocker.

Despite their glamorous looks, American cockers were originally bred from English cocker spaniels, dogs that are built for running through fields to find birds. This means that American cockers are busy characters who need lots of exercise and playtime, as well as daily brushing to keep that coat looking its best. Upbeat, sweet and snuggly, these pretty dogs make loving family pets.

POOCH PROFILE:
Country: USA **Size:** Small; 34–39 cm (13–15 in) tall **Coat:** Long coat; comes in a wide variety of colours, including black, chocolate, red, black and tan, tricolour **Personality:** Gentle, merry, faithful

Round head

Large, round eyes

Soft expression

Long hair on ears

Whippy tail that waves happily when on the move

Silky coat

AMERICAN WATER SPANIEL

The American water spaniel is a very different kind of spaniel. First bred in and around the Great Lakes of the American Midwest, this all-weather dog is happiest diving into icy water after a duck or swimming alongside a boat.

Energetic and practical, these dogs are the ultimate outdoor-activity companions. However, you'll be lucky to spot one outside of the USA and they're a rare breed in their home country, with only an estimated 3,000 around today.

POOCH PROFILE:
Country: USA **Size:** Small–Medium; 38–45 cm (15–18 in) tall **Coat:** Medium-length coat with a wavy or curly texture; brown **Personality:** Active, eager, happy

Fairly small body (good for jumping in and out of boats)

Wavy or tightly curled waterproof coat

Thick paw pads

Brown fur

Webbed feet

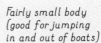

Broad head

Longer muzzle than
other bulldog breeds

Short, smooth
coat

Muscly body

Long legs

AMERICAN BULLDOG

The American bulldog was bred from dogs that were brought to the USA by European settlers in the 1800s. Energetic and strong, American bulldogs were perfect for life on farms and ranches, where they helped with jobs such as herding cattle and hunting.

Although they look chunky, American bulldogs are athletes and need plenty of exercise to keep them happy. With good training, they make extremely loyal, goofy pets and brilliant jogging buddies.

POOCH PROFILE:
Country: USA **Size:** Large; 51–64 cm (20–25 in) tall **Coat:** Short and smooth; usually white with patches of black, brown or brindle **Personality:** Loyal, energetic, protective

AUSTRALIAN SHEPHERD

Despite their name, 'Aussies' are now an all-American dog. Their ancestors were collie-type dogs that were taken from Europe to America (with a stop-off in Australia) by Spanish settlers in the 19th century. Smart, and quick on their feet, the dogs turned out to be the perfect partners for cowboys on ranches in California.

Like their collie cousins, Australian shepherds are devoted companions who need to have a job to do to keep them happy. A pet Aussie will never get bored of learning new tricks, from shaking a paw and rolling over, to dancing and even yoga! Intelligent and eager to please, they also make excellent assistance, therapy and search-and-rescue dogs.

POOCH PROFILE:
Country: USA **Size:** Medium–Large; 46–58 cm (18–23 in) tall **Coat:** Medium-length, wavy coat; black, blue merle, red merle, red **Personality:** Hard-working, super-smart, loyal

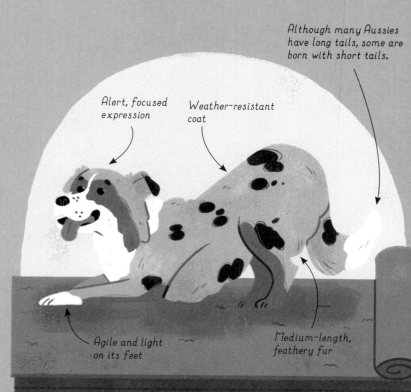

Although many Aussies
have long tails, some are
born with short tails.

Alert, focused
expression

Weather-resistant
coat

Agile and light
on its feet

Medium-length,
feathery fur

BLACK-AND-TAN COONHOUND

Coonhounds are a group of North American scenthounds that were bred for their incredible sense of smell. There are several different breeds of coonhound, but the black-and-tan coonhound is one of the best-known outside the USA.

These skilful hunting dogs are famous for having a 'cold nose', meaning they can follow a trail even if there's hardly any scent left. Alert when out and about (squirrels, beware!), they are also happy chilling in a comfy bed for hours. Like many hounds, these dogs were bred to have strong howls to attract the attention of their humans when out hunting, so they love the sound of their own voice. If a black-and-tan is living in your neighbourhood, you'll know about it!

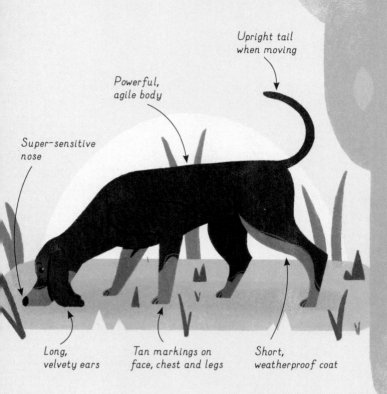

Upright tail when moving

Powerful, agile body

Super-sensitive nose

Long, velvety ears

Tan markings on face, chest and legs

Short, weatherproof coat

POOCH PROFILE:
Country: USA **Size:** Large; 58–69 cm (23–27 in) tall **Coat:** Short; black-and-tan colour
Personality: Friendly, alert, easy-going

MOUNTAIN CUR

Curs are a group of American hounds that specialise in chasing their prey up trees. A breed called mountain curs are the descendants of dogs that were brought by European settlers to the hilly southern regions of America in the 1800s. They acted as guard dogs, hunting dogs and family companions, helping people survive in tough conditions.

Mountain curs are courageous and clever dogs that must be given tasks to do to channel their energy, such as agility or scent games. Bred to survive in rugged mountains, they need a lot of space and exercise to keep them happy.

Intelligent expression

Folded ears

Thick but short coat

Sturdy body

Long legs

POOCH PROFILE:
Country: USA **Size:** Medium–Large; 41–66 cm (16–26 in) tall **Coat:** Short coat; can be black, brown, brindle, blue, red, yellow, sometimes with white markings **Personality:** Brave, intelligent, active

LITTLE DOGS

From Mexico's Chihuahua (p24) to China's pug (p90), some of the world's most popular pooches come in tiny packages. Many small dogs belong to the 'toy' group – dogs that have been bred to put their paws up and chill out with people. But just because they are cute and cuddly, that doesn't mean they are any less dog. These furballs need a lot of care, love and exercise to keep them happy.

POMERANIAN (Germany)

Size: 22–28 cm (9–11 in) tall
Pomeranians are the smallest type of spitz – dogs with thick coats and pointy ears and noses – and were originally bred from much larger dogs. Confident and lively, Poms have the character of a big dog and love to use their busy brain to master tricks such as shaking a paw or spinning.

GRIFFON BRUXELLOIS (Belgium)

Size: 23–28 cm (9–11 in) tall
Griffs were originally used as watchdogs in stables before becoming a favourite breed of the Belgian queen, Marie Henriette, in the 19th century. They've been living in the lap of luxury ever since. With big moustaches and a monkey-like expression, they make lively, cheeky companions.

RUSSIAN TOY (Russia)

Size: 20–28 cm (8–11 in) tall
This dainty breed was a rat-catcher before becoming a lapdog for Russian aristocrats in the 18th century. Russian toys are happy to snuggle up to you but will also enjoy a good run around on their long legs. They have large, bat-like ears and can have smooth or long coats.

TOY SPANIELS (UK)

Size: Cavalier King Charles spaniels are 30–33 cm (12–13 in) tall; King Charles spaniels are 25–27 cm (10–11 in) tall
Toy spaniels were originally bred to be the lapdogs of kings. There are two breeds – the Cavalier King Charles spaniel and the King Charles spaniel (left). Both breeds have long, feathery ears, soulful eyes and gentle characters. The Cavalier is slightly larger, while the smaller King Charles has a flatter face.

BICHON FRISE (France/Mediterranean)

Size: 23–28 cm (9–11 in) tall
The bichon frise belongs to a group of little white dogs that originally came from the Mediterranean region. With cloud-like curls – their name means 'small curly-haired dog' – bright black eyes and a happy-go-lucky attitude, bichons frises are some of the stylish dogs on the block. And they know it!

CHIHUAHUA

The tiniest dogs in the world, Chihuahuas are one of the oldest breeds of the Americas. What Chihuahuas lack in size, they make up for in attitude – big time! They're clever, curious and brave characters that like to be top dog. They're also enthusiastic and surprisingly loud watchdogs.

Chihuahuas are very easy to carry around – and that's how they like it. They want to be with you all day, every day, and often get very attached to one person. Although they're happy to watch the world go by from your lap, Chihuahuas are brainy dogs that will enjoy being taught tricks and even take part in agility or obedience competitions.

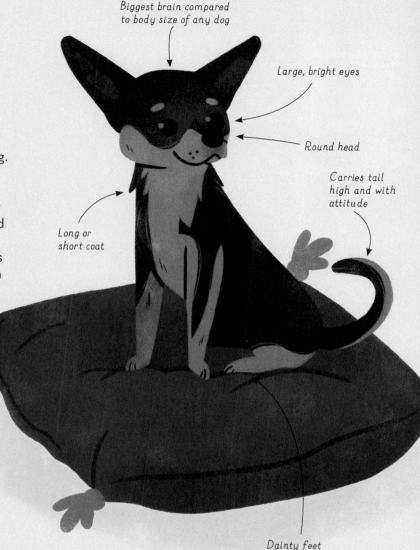

Biggest brain compared to body size of any dog

Large, bright eyes

Round head

Carries tail high and with attitude

Long or short coat

Dainty feet

Chihuahuas are named after an area of Mexico, but their exact origins are uncertain. They're thought to be descended from an extinct breed called Techichi, which was treasured by the ancient Toltec and Aztec people. Just like their ancestors, Chihuahuas love to be worshipped!

POOCH PROFILE:
Country: Mexico **Size:** Tiny; 12–20 cm (5–8 in) tall
Coat: Short- or long-haired; various colours including black, black and tan, chocolate, cream, tricolour **Personality:** Bold, smart, fun-loving

XOLOITZCUINTLI

Xoloitzcuintli (you say it 'show-low-eats-queen-tlee') – or Xolos ('show-lows') for short – are an ancient breed from the Americas. These rare, usually hairless dogs have been around for at least 3,000 years and were named after Xolotl, the Aztec god of the underworld. Treasured by the Aztecs, the dogs were believed to guard the living and protect souls in the afterlife.

'Hairless dogs of the underworld' may not sound very cuddly, but Xolos are an affectionate, faithful breed who love to be around people. They also feel weirdly warm – apparently, the Aztecs tucked Xolos into bed alongside ill people to soothe aches and pains, a bit like a hot-water bottle!

Large, pointy ears

Hairless dogs may still have tufts of hair on head and tail

Wrinkled brow

Almond-shaped eyes

Long neck

Long, slim tail

POOCH PROFILE:
Country: Mexico **Size:** Toy is 25–35 cm (10–14 in); Miniature is 36–45 cm (14–18 in); Standard is 46–60 cm (18–23 in) tall **Coat:** Can be coated or hairless; various colours including black, brown, tan and white **Personality:** Loyal, elegant, sensitive

HAVANESE

Bright as buttons and with bubbly personalities to match, Havanese are brilliant family dogs. Their sunny personalities match the climate of their home nation of Cuba, where they are the national dog.

It's thought their ancestors were bichon-type dogs (p23) that were brought to the Cuban city of Havana by Spanish or Italian merchants in the 1600s. Over the centuries, these dogs were crossed with poodles to create a super-cute and clever pooch that comes in a variety of colours. The ultimate companion dog, Havanese are happiest when they're by your side.

Hair grows long and fluffy – but Havanese look just as sweet with a shorter hairdo

Bright, gentle expression

Silky coat

Curled-over tail

Fairly sturdy body

POOCH PROFILE:
Country: Cuba **Size:** Small; 23–28 cm (9–11 in) tall **Coat:** Soft and silky; can be any colour, including black, cream, red or black and white **Personality:** Friendly, confident, clever

The Peruvian hairless dog is known by lots of different names, including the Peruvian viringo and the moonflower dog. The dogs are said to have first been given flowery nicknames by Spanish conquistadors, who found them living among orchid plants. The Peruvian Inca Orchid is a modern version of the breed developed in the USA in the 1960s and named by an American breeder.

BRAZILIAN TERRIER
BRAZIL

Pictures of Peruvian hairless dogs have been found on pots dating back to 750 CE.

PERUVIAN HAIRLESS DOG
PERU

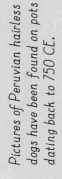

CHILEAN TERRIER
CHILE

MUCUCHI
VENEZUELA

Mucuchíes have a special place in Venezuelan history thanks to a dog called Nevado, who stood by the side of his owner, the political leader Simón Bolívar, during the country's fight for independence in the early 1800s.

Chilean terriers are often born with no tail, or a very short bobtail.

SOUTH AMERICA

If you meet a dog in South America, chances are they belong to one of two groups. There are ancient hairless dogs that have lived on the continent for thousands of years, and there are dogs that were introduced by European settlers in the last few hundred years. You'll be lucky to bump into any of these breeds outside of South America, as most of these dogs are not very well known beyond their home countries. Get set to meet some of the most rare and unusual doggos on the planet.

ARGENTINE PILA DOG
ARGENTINA

If you go to a museum in Peru, you won't just see dogs on pots! In 2001, the Peruvian government announced that every archaeological museum along Peru's coast must have a pair of Peruvian hairless dogs living on site.

PATAGONIAN SHEEPDOG
CHILE

To keep their Patagonian sheepdogs in tip-top condition, farmers often trim their coats at the same time as they shear their sheep!

Patagonian sheepdogs are so skilled at herding that it's estimated just one dog can control a flock of 300 sheep!

PERUVIAN HAIRLESS DOG

These hairless hounds were once the cherished companions of Peru's ancient civilizations. They appear on pottery and textiles that date back thousands of years, where they are shown as faithful friends and symbols of good luck and are sometimes even wearing jumpers.

When European settlers arrived in Peru in the 1500s, they thought the dogs were ugly and scary. Because of this, the breed started to die off and only a small number were left in remote mountain villages. Things changed in the 1990s when fans saved the breed. Nowadays, these wrinkly pooches are loved and protected across Peru. The national dog of Peru, they even have their own day on 12th June.

POOCH PROFILE:
Country: Peru **Size:** Small is 25–41 cm (10–16 in) tall; Medium is 40–50 cm (16–20 in) tall; Large is 50–65 cm (20–26 in) tall **Coat:** Usually hairless but can have fur; variety of colours including black, brown, cream with pink patches **Personality:** Graceful, alert, good-natured

Pointy ears

Hairless dogs still sometimes have tufts of hair on their heads.

Slim body

Can be hairless or coated

Peruvian hairless dogs behave a lot like sighthounds such as greyhounds and whippets. They're energetic and love to chase anything small and furry. Although they're a bit standoffish with people they don't know, these dogs are very loyal and happiest when with their human pack.

HAIRLESS HOUNDS

Peru's smooth-skinned pooches are the only official hairless breed of South America. But fur-free dogs are also found in many other countries on the continent – from the Ecuadorian hairless dog to the Argentine pila dog and the Bolivian hairless dog. Experts aren't sure whether these dogs are different breeds or just Peruvian hairless dogs living in different countries.

Wherever they come from, all hairless dogs can be sensitive to big changes in temperature. Doggie sun cream is a must on very hot days, especially if a hairless dog has pale skin. These dogs will also be glad of a cosy jacket in winter.

POOCH PROFILE:

Country: Found across South America **Size:** Small, medium or large **Coat:** Usually hairless but can have fur **Personality:** Affectionate and loyal

Hairless dogs have a special gene that means they are born without fur. Although the hair-free versions are the most well-known, all of these South American dogs appear in furry varieties as well, and there can be a mix of hairy and non-hairy pups in one litter. Even bald pups can still have wisps of hair. They often have hairy heads (like doggie mohicans), or feathery tufts on their feet and tail.

GENTLE GIANTS

If you like big cuddles (and a lot of slobber), look no further than these gigantic dogs. Many big breeds come from mountainous regions of the world, where they were originally used to guard farm animals or rescue people. Others have ancient roots as warriors or guard dogs. Whatever their background, one thing is for certain – each of these super-sized softies will need a sofa all to themselves!

GREAT DANE (Germany)

Size: 71–81 cm (28–32 in) tall
Despite their name, these dogs originally came from Germany, where they were used as hunting and guard dogs. They're the giants of the dog world – when a Great Dane stands on its back legs, it's taller than most people. They have big hearts to match their heft and make very soppy, affectionate pets.

ST BERNARD (Switzerland)

Size: 71–76 cm (28–30 in) tall
The national dog of Switzerland, St Bernards are famous for their bravery and gentleness. Bred to rescue people lost in the Swiss mountains, these dogs have powerful bodies for trudging through snowstorms and a courageous, kindly nature.

PYRENEAN MOUNTAIN DOG (France)

Size: 65–70 cm (26–28 in) tall
These enormous fluffballs have been guarding sheep in the Pyrenees mountains for hundreds of years. Built to take on bears and wolves, they are very strong dogs, but have calm, steady personalities, and nowadays, they're just as happy chilling out with their human flock.

According to the Guinness World Records, the tallest dog ever was a Great Dane called Zeus. This super-sized pooch measured 1.118 m (3.66 ft) from his foot to his shoulder, and was 2.23 m (7.31 ft) tall when he stood on his back legs.

The record for the longest and heaviest dog ever is held by Zorba, a mastiff. Zorba had a nose to tail length of 2.544 m (8.346 ft) and weighed a mighty 156.5 kg (345 lbs).

MASTIFF (UK)

Size: 70–77 cm (28–30 in) tall
These colossal dogs are the largest breed by weight – they can weigh as much as 104 kg (229 lbs), which is heavier than many human grown-ups! With massive heads and booming barks, they can seem intimidating, but with good training mastiffs make faithful, lovable pets, guaranteed to slobber all over you.

NEAPOLITAN MASTIFF (Italy)

Size: 60–75 cm (24–30 in) tall
This ancient Italian breed is said to have led Roman armies into battle. Chunky and powerful, Neos are built to protect and bond very closely to their humans. You might recognise these wrinkly faces from the big screen – in the Harry Potter films, Hagrid's pooch pal Fang is played by a Neapolitan mastiff.

TIBETAN MASTIFF (China)

Size: 61–76 cm (24–30 in) tall
This bear-like dog is thought to be the ancestor of all the mastiffs and is one of the oldest breeds in the world. Tibetan mastiffs have muscly bodies and very thick, woolly coats to help them survive the harsh winters of the Himalayas.

PATAGONIAN SHEEPDOG

The windy plains of Patagonia in southern Chile are home to a rare and little-known dog. Covered from nose to tail in thick fur, Patagonian sheepdogs look a bit like scruffy teddy bears. But underneath those shaggy coats are strong working dogs that can tough it out on cold winter nights and run for miles to round up lost sheep.

In the 1800s, European settlers discovered that Patagonia's lush grasslands were perfect for sheep farming. This meant that many farmers from Europe came there to make their fortune, and they brought their dogs along for the ride. These sheepdogs were some of the best in the business – such as border collies (p60), bearded collies and the now-extinct old Welsh grey. Over the years, the dogs bred together to make the Patagonian sheepdogs of today.

Intelligent and alert expression

Some dogs have pointed ears, others have floppier ears.

Medium-length to long coat that comes in a variety of colours

Fur is thick to protect from the cold

Long legs – these dogs are fast!

POOCH PROFILE:

Country: Chile **Size:** Large; 50–55 cm (19–22 in) tall **Coat:** Medium-length to long; comes in a variety of colours **Personality:** Hard-working, agile, intelligent

Calm, steady expression

Triangular ears

Wedge-shaped head

Broad back

Feathery tail

Sturdy body

Very dense fur that is straight or slightly wavy

Large, strong paws

MUCUCHÍ

Mucuchíes ('moo-coo-chis') take their cuddly-sounding name from a town in the Andes mountains, where these mighty dogs have been used to herd and guard sheep for centuries. They are believed to be descended from dogs that were brought to Venezuela by Spanish settlers – possibly the Pyrenean mountain dog (p30) and Spanish mastiff. Like these European breeds, Mucuchíes are hardy and hard-working, with thick coats to keep out the cold. Venezuela's only native breed, these fluffballs have been the country's national dog since 1964.

POOCH PROFILE:

Country: Venezuela **Size:** Large–Giant; 56–71 cm (22–28 in) tall **Coat:** Thick and dense; usually white with honey-brown patches or black spots **Personality:** Active, intelligent, affectionate

CHILEAN TERRIER

Perky ears (These dogs have excellent hearing.)

Bright expression

Often born with a short tail

Smooth, short coat

All-white fur, apart from markings on the head and, sometimes, on the back

Some dogs living in colder regions can develop an undercoat.

Chilean terriers were developed by British settlers in the 1800s who crossed smooth-coated fox terriers with local dogs. The result was this hardy breed, which looks very similar to a fox terrier but is better suited to the hot and cold climates found in Chile.

Although these terriers were first used to catch rats on farms and in cities, today they make popular pets across Chile. Despite their small size, they are plucky watchdogs and will always let you know when the postman's at the door. But they are also said to be slightly more laid back than your average terrier and will happily snuggle in your lap after a good run with a tennis ball.

POOCH PROFILE:
Country: Chile **Size:** Small; 28–35 cm (11–15 in) tall **Coat:** Smooth, short fur; mainly white with tricolour markings on head and back **Personality:** Adaptable, playful, active

BRAZILIAN TERRIER

How these dogs got to Brazil is a bit of a mystery. They're thought to either be the descendants of British terriers, such as Jack Russells (p54), or Spanish breeds, like the Ratonero Bodeguero Andaluz, which were taken to South America by European settlers. Although they have playful and friendly characters, these feisty pups were originally bred to catch rats on farms, so they like to be kept active and busy. Oh, and they also love to dig!

POOCH PROFILE:
Country: Brazil **Size:** Small; 33–40 cm (13–16 in) tall **Coat:** Short and smooth; tricolour pattern **Personality:** Alert, spirited, bold

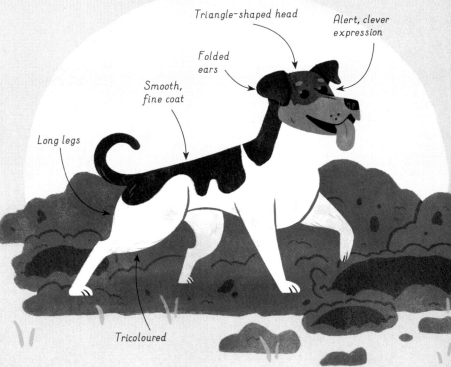

Triangle-shaped head

Alert, clever expression

Folded ears

Smooth, fine coat

Long legs

Tricoloured

DOGGIE DICTIONARY

Dogs are tuned in to how we feel – they can sense our feelings, read our faces and even follow our hand signals. It's part of what makes the bond between humans and dogs so special. But we're not always so good at reading their language. We humans rely a lot on speech to find out what other people are thinking. Dogs use noises and their sense of smell to communicate with each other (see pp10–11), but they mainly use their bodies to tell us how they're feeling. Here are some basics to help you understand what your four-legged friend is trying to say.

TAIL TALK

It might sound weird, but a waggy tail doesn't always mean a dog is happy. The speed of the wag can reveal a lot about how a dog is feeling. A quick, twitchy wag can mean that a dog is alert or even anxious about a situation. A slow, gentle wag is usually the happy and relaxed one. When a dog greets you with a tail that spins all the way round in a circle (nicknamed a 'helicopter wag'), it is *extremely* happy – these sort of wags are usually reserved for special friends.

The way a dog holds its tail can also give you a clue about its feelings. But this can vary from breed to breed, as some dogs have more naturally upright tails than others.

A tail held loosely in a neutral position, maybe with a gentle wag, means the dog is calm.

Broad wags from side to side mean the dog is happy.

A stiff, upright tail means the dog is on the alert.

Tail tucked between legs or pointing straight down means the dog is nervous.

BODY BASICS

Just as we might slump our shoulders when we're sad or walk tall when we're happy, the way in which a dog holds its body can say a lot about its emotions. When it is feeling excited and playful, you might see it do a 'play bow' – this is when a dog puts its chest on the ground, bum in the air and wiggles its tail happily (1). When a dog is alert or anxious, its body usually goes rigid and still. At the same time, it might raise one paw off the ground (2). This means 'I'm uncertain'.

LOOK INTO MY EYES...

A dog's eyes can tell you a lot about its mood. Soft eyes – which sometimes look like a squint – mean a dog is relaxed (1), whereas a hard, staring look usually means a dog is alert or guarding something (2). If a dog is showing you the white part of their eyes (sometimes called 'whale eye'), they may be feeling uncomfortable (3). For example, they might be being stroked by someone they don't know and want you to either rescue them or let them know it's okay.

01

02

03

FACE TIME

Some expressions can be harder to read than others. A dog that is licking its lips may have just gobbled up a treat, but dogs also lick their lips when they feel worried. These anxious licks are normally small and quick – they're unlike a laid-back 'Yum, breakfast!' lick. In the same way, a yawn can indicate sleepiness, but dogs also yawn to calm themselves when they feel stressed – and say 'Don't mind me, I am not a threat' to whatever is stressing them out.

HAND SIGNALS

Studies have shown that dogs can follow what we humans are thinking just by watching our hand gestures. In fact, dogs have been shown to understand and interpret our hand signals far better than chimpanzees, our nearest animal relatives.

Finnish spitzes are super woofers! Some have been recorded hitting an astonishing 160 barks per minute.

1. **NORWEGIAN ELKHOUND** NORWAY
2. **HAMILTONSTOVARE** SWEDEN
3. **FINNISH SPITZ** FINLAND
4. **OLD ENGLISH SHEEPDOG** UK (ENGLAND)
5. **ENGLISH SPRINGER SPANIEL** UK (ENGLAND)
6. **BULLDOG** UK (ENGLAND)
7. **GREYHOUND** UK (ENGLAND)
8. **WIRE FOX TERRIER** UK (ENGLAND)
9. **YORKSHIRE TERRIER** UK (ENGLAND)
10. **WELSH CORGIS** UK (WALES)
11. **GOLDEN RETRIEVER** UK (SCOTLAND)
12. **SCOTTISH TERRIER** UK (SCOTLAND)
13. **IRISH WOLFHOUND** IRELAND
14. **IRISH SETTER** IRELAND
15. **FRENCH BULLDOG** FRANCE
16. **PAPILLON** FRANCE
17. **POODLE** FRANCE/GERMANY
18. **BASSET HOUND** FRANCE
19. **BELGIAN SHEPHERD DOGS** BELGIUM
20. **BERNESE MOUNTAIN DOG** SWITZERLAND
21. **KEESHOND** NETHERLANDS
22. **SCHNAUZER** GERMANY
23. **DACHSHUND** GERMANY
24. **WEIMARANER** GERMANY
25. **BOXER** GERMANY
26. **ROTTWEILER** GERMANY
27. **GERMAN SHEPHERD** GERMANY

EUROPE (North/West)

Europe may not be home to breeds as ancient as those of South America or Africa, but it's the continent where the majority of modern dogs were born. From the petite papillon to the enormous Irish wolfhound, the dogs of western Europe alone come in an incredible range of shapes and sizes. Although many started out as specialist sheepdogs, mighty mountaineers or tenacious trackers, today they can be found snuggling on sofas the world over.

23.

The bushy beard of a schnauzer isn't just for show. One of a schnauzer's original jobs was to hunt rats and other rodents, and their thick moustaches protected the dogs from being bitten.

22.

20.

24.

17.

15.

16.

18.

Papillons are one of the oldest toy breeds. We know these dainty dogs have been sitting in the lap of luxury since at least the 1500s because they pop up in paintings by the famous Italian artist, Titian.

Although basset hounds are short dogs, they are surprisingly hefty. They can weigh up to 30 kg (65 lbs) – almost three times the weight of a similarly sausage-shaped dog, the dachshund.

Tightly curled tail which rolls over the back

Handsome, silvery coat

Pointy ears

Confident, friendly expression

Compact, sturdy body

Very thick, soft and weather-resistant fur

POOCH PROFILE:
Country: Norway **Size:** Large; 49–52 cm (19–20 in) tall **Coat:** Thick and soft; various shades of silvery-grey, darker around face, on ears and on the tips of the topcoat **Personality:** Playful, intelligent, brave

NORWEGIAN ELKHOUND

A helper to Stone Age hunters and friend to the Vikings, this fearless, affectionate dog has been by the side of humans for thousands of years. Elkhounds feature in Norse legends and still hold an important place in the culture of Norway, where they are the national breed.

These dogs have a lot of energy and an independent streak – if they smell a fox in the park, they are guaranteed to run off after it! An elkhound's original job was to track down elk and other large animals, such as bears. They were also used to herd and guard farms. Their loud bark – which they used to get the attention of their humans on a hunt – makes elkhounds effective watchdogs, if rather noisy housemates. But if you love being outdoors and don't mind a woofer, you couldn't want for a truer companion.

HAMILTONSTOVARE

In the 1800s, a Swedish noble (and dog-enthusiast) called Count Hamilton wanted to create a hound that could sniff out and catch hares and foxes. It's thought that he crossed English hounds – probably foxhounds – with German hounds to create the Hamiltonstovare.

Unlike foxhounds, which like to be part of a pack, Hamiltonstovares were bred to hunt alone. They are also unusual among hounds in being as skilled at picking out an unsuspecting critter by sight as well as by smell. Although they're energetic, these even-tempered dogs are happy to laze around at home with you, too.

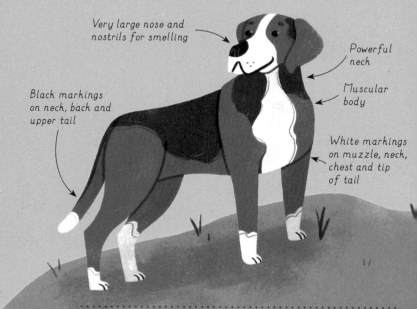

Very large nose and nostrils for smelling

Powerful neck

Muscular body

Black markings on neck, back and upper tail

White markings on muzzle, neck, chest and tip of tail

POOCH PROFILE:
Country: Sweden **Size:** Large; 49–61 cm (19–23 in) tall **Coat:** Short; black, white and tan pattern **Personality:** Friendly, agile, dignified

Sharply pointed ears

Wedge-shaped head

Topcoat is dense and long, especially around tail and back legs

Fluffy tail that curls over the back

Deep red fur

Strong, straight front legs

Light, bouncy walk

FINNISH SPITZ

With a flame-red coat and fox-like features, there's no mistaking the Finnish spitz. These stunning dogs have a spirit that's as fiery as their fur colour. They are active, outgoing, quick-witted pooches … and they like to make themselves heard!

The national dog of Finland, these hounds are used in their homeland to hunt birds in thick forests. When it finds its prey, a Finnish spitz sways its fluffy tail to distract the bird, and uses its yodel-like bark to alert its humans. These dogs love the sound of their own voice, so much so that, in Finland, yearly competitions are held to crown a 'King of the Barkers' – the dog who can keep barking for the longest time wins!

Finnish spitzes have a short, dense undercoat and a longer topcoat to keep them warm through Finland's long winters. When they shed their undercoat (usually twice a year), a daily brush will help remove excess fur. The rest of the time, a good brush each week will keep them looking their foxy best.

POOCH PROFILE:

Country: Finland **Size:** Medium; 39–50 cm (15–20 in) tall **Coat:** Long on body and back legs, shorter on front and head; red **Personality:** Smart, vocal, lively

OLD ENGLISH SHEEPDOG

With their shaggy, panda-patterned coat, the Old English sheepdog is one of the UK's most distinctive breeds. Despite sounding as English as a cup of tea, the breed is thought to be the result of crossing Scottish and European herding dogs and was first developed in the 1700s.

Their fabulous fluffiness has made these dogs popular in show rings, but they are more than just puffballs. Beneath all that hair is a powerful, intelligent worker, whose original job was to help guide cattle along the road to market – not herd sheep, as the name suggests. Old English sheepdogs are extremely sweet and affectionate, particularly with kids, and make wonderful family pets … as long as you're prepared for a serious amount of brushing!

POOCH PROFILE:

Country: UK **Size:** Large; generally 56–61 cm (22–24 in) tall but can be bigger **Coat:** Long and thick; grey or grey-blue and white **Personality:** Gentle, trustworthy, bold

Large, square head

Dense coat with a rough texture

Pear-shaped body

Sturdy legs

Has a rolling, bear-like walk

Nimble feet with thick, hard paw pads

ENGLISH SPRINGER SPANIEL

Springer spaniels get their name from the way they startle (or 'spring') birds hiding in undergrowth. Originally used by English hunters in the 1800s, today these sprightly pooches make popular pets, as well as excellent sniffer dogs, thanks to their trainability and sharp sense of smell.

Like most spaniels, a springer is a sweet, friendly dog, constantly wagging its tail. Built for running around fields day after day, springers like an outdoorsy, busy life. They will happily spend an afternoon playing fetch with you without tiring – or losing any enthusiasm!

POOCH PROFILE:

Country: UK **Size:** Medium; 51 cm (20 in) tall **Coat:** Medium-length, straight fur; liver and white, black and white or tricolour **Personality:** Playful, active, eager to please

Long ears, with feathery fur

Gentle expression

Feathery tail that wags in a lively way

Long, strong neck

Deep chest

Straight fur

BULLDOG

Snoring in an armchair, with its rolls of skin smooshed against a cushion, a modern bulldog seems very different from its fierce ancestors. The original bulldogs were used in a cruel 'sport' known as bull baiting, in which a dog was encouraged to attack a bull. After bull baiting was banned in the UK in 1835, the breed faced extinction but was saved by fans who created today's gentle, popular pet.

Bulldogs make loving, loyal companions, but they do need special care: their flat face and large, heavy head means they can become short of breath, particularly on a hot day. They may also struggle to cope with lots of stairs due to their chunky build.

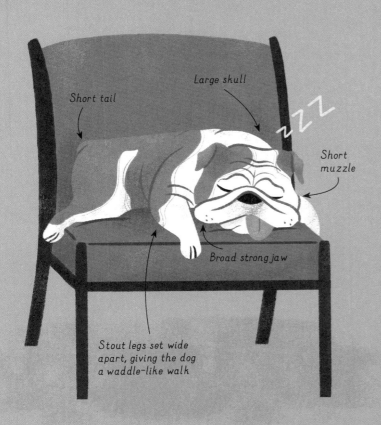

Short tail

Large skull

Short muzzle

Broad strong jaw

Stout legs set wide apart, giving the dog a waddle-like walk

POOCH PROFILE:
Country: UK **Size:** Medium; 38–40 cm (15–16 in) tall **Coat:** Short and smooth; normally white with fawn, red or brindle patches
Personality: Friendly, laid-back, courageous

GREYHOUND

Greyhounds were first developed in England during the Middle Ages to chase and catch wild animals, mainly hares. These speedy dogs were so prized that a law was passed to say that only royals and nobles could hunt with them.

POOCH PROFILE:
Country: UK **Size:** Large; 69–76 cm (27–30 in) tall **Coat:** Very short; comes in a variety of colours, including black, white, red and brindle
Personality: Gentle, graceful, super-fast

Greyhounds are 'sighthounds', meaning they use their eyes (rather than their nose) to find prey and then run after it. They have streamlined bodies to help them cover ground quickly and can reach speeds of 70 km (43.5 miles) per hour, making them the fastest dog in the world. A zooming greyhound will strike fear into the heart of any small, furry animal, but these dogs actually make very chilled-out pets. If you let a greyhound into your life, be prepared to share your sofa with it – they are complete couch potatoes!

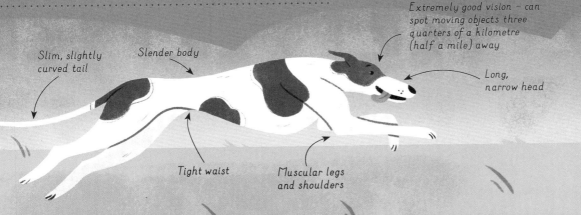

Slim, slightly curved tail

Slender body

Extremely good vision – can spot moving objects three quarters of a kilometre (half a mile) away

Long, narrow head

Tight waist

Muscular legs and shoulders

WIRE FOX TERRIER

When one of these dogs walks into a room, you'll know about it. With their brisk, tippy-toe trot and teddy-bear looks, wire fox terriers are the showmen of the dog world. So much so, they are often used in films and on TV. One dog actor called Skippy, whose tricks included howling on command and doing a backflip, was in such demand in Hollywood in the 1930s that he was paid $200 (£148) a week – more than $3,000 (£2,225) in today's money!

The origins of these sparky dogs are less glamorous. They were developed in the 1700s to chase, or more often dig, a fox out of its burrow during a hunt. They still love to dig and will happily treat your garden as a giant sandpit if given the chance. To avoid this, they need to be kept busy. Games with a tuggy toy will do, but, as Skippy shows, these clever dogs are capable of learning lots of tricks if you put in the time.

Dark eyes with a fiercely intelligent expression

Long, sloping face

Upright tail

Crisp, dense hair

Compact, sleek body

Straight legs

Round, small feet

POOCH PROFILE:

Country: UK (England) **Size:** Small; 39 cm (15 in) tall **Coat:** Very wiry; white with black and/or tan markings **Personality:** Bright, inquisitive, fearless

Straight, glossy coat

Small, slightly flat head

V-shaped ears

Sparkling, alert eyes

Compact body

YORKSHIRE TERRIER

A Yorkshire terrier with lush, silky locks and a bow on its head is a familiar sight in a show ring. But although they are petted and pampered today, these little dogs were originally bred for a tough day's work hunting rats in coal mines and cotton mills in the north of England. Throw a squeaky toy for a Yorkie and you'll see their true colours!

Yorkshire terriers have very fine hair, which needs a huge amount of daily care and brushing if it is left to grow long. Most pet Yorkies have a shorter 'puppy cut' which is more practical for day-to-day activities. Although they will happily watch the world go by from your lap, these dogs are feisty and smart and will delight in a routine that includes plenty of playtime as well as cuddles.

POOCH PROFILE:

Country: UK **Size:** Tiny; 17–20 cm (7–8 in) tall **Coat:** Long and straight; steel-blue and tan markings **Personality:** Confident, brave, loving

WELSH CORGIS
(Pembroke and Cardigan)

These dogs may look dumpy but don't be fooled! For at least a thousand years, corgis have been fixtures on Welsh farms where they specialised in nipping at the heels of cattle to move them along, as well as acting as all-round workers and watchdogs.

There are two breeds of corgis – the Pembroke Welsh corgi and the Cardigan Welsh corgi (named after neighbouring counties in Wales). Although they look similar, they have very different origins. The Cardigan is thought to be descended from dogs who came to Britain with the Celts in around 1200 BCE, while the Pembroke's ancestors were the dogs of Belgian weavers and farmers who arrived in Wales in the Middle Ages.

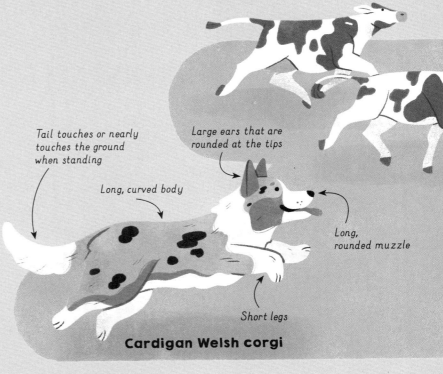

Tail touches or nearly touches the ground when standing

Large ears that are rounded at the tips

Long, curved body

Long, rounded muzzle

Short legs

Cardigan Welsh corgi

Pointed, foxy ears

Rectangular shape

Pointed muzzle

Curved tail

Short legs

Pembroke Welsh corgi

POOCH PROFILE:
Country: UK **Size:** Small; Pembrokes are 25–30 cm (10–12 in) tall; Cardigans are 28–30 cm (11–12 in) tall **Coat:** Medium-length fur with dense undercoat. Pembrokes are usually red or fawn with white markings; Cardigans come in a variety of colours, including brindle and blue merle. **Personality:** Friendly, athletic, alert

Today, the Pembroke corgi is more associated with palaces than farmyards. These spirited pooches with foxy-looking faces are a favourite dog of Queen Elizabeth II – who even snuck her beloved Pembroke corgi, Susan, into her carriage on her wedding day. Cardigan corgis have a more rugged appearance, with a longer nose and body, a brush-like tail and often a brindle or blue-merle coat.

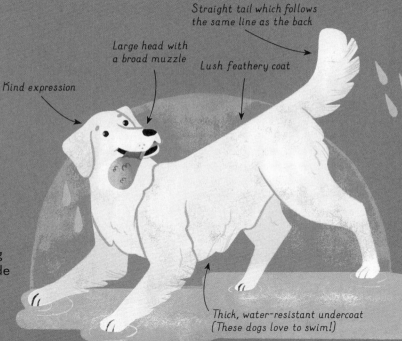

Straight tail which follows the same line as the back

Large head with a broad muzzle

Lush feathery coat

Kind expression

Thick, water-resistant undercoat (These dogs love to swim!)

GOLDEN RETRIEVER

Golden retrievers (or 'goldens') were developed in the 1800s by crossing black retrievers, spaniels, setters and bloodhounds to create a dog suited to the wet, wild climate of the Scottish Highlands. They can turn their talents to pretty much anything, from assisting blind people to helping sniff out explosives. Their beauty and kind natures have made them one of the most popular family dogs in the world.

Built for romping round mountains, goldens are active dogs that need at least two hours of exercise a day. They have a cheeky, puppyish attitude till they are about three years old, and even older goldens have moments of pup-like silliness, so they need plenty of playtime. They also love being given tasks to do and their soft mouths are perfectly designed for fetching things, from footballs to your slippers.

POOCH PROFILE:

Country: UK (Scotland) **Size:** Large; 51–61 cm (20–24 in) tall **Coat:** Medium-length, flat or wavy fur; either cream or gold in colour **Personality:** Clever, affectionate, trustworthy

Alert, pricked-up ears

SCOTTISH TERRIER

With a coal-black coat, bushy beard and extreme eyebrows, the Scottish terrier has a look all of its own. Often paired with a tartan collar, this solid, dignified dog is an icon of its home country, where it was first developed to hunt foxes and badgers in the Highlands.

Scotties are little dogs with very strong characters. They have a brisk, business-like walk, which suggests they have an important job to do, and they take their duties as a watchdog and companion super-seriously. Their independence and gruff manner can make them seem a little aloof towards people they don't know, but if you make friends with a Scottie, they'll have your back for life.

Strong, muscular neck

Wiry topcoat, soft undercoat

Upright tail

Long face with lush beard and eyebrows

Short legs, with extremely powerful back legs for a small dog

POOCH PROFILE:

Country: UK (Scotland) **Size:** Small; 25–28 cm (10–11 in) tall **Coat:** Dense coat; normally black, but can also be brindle and wheaten **Personality:** Independent, bold, brave

IRISH WOLFHOUND

The mighty Irish wolfhound towers above all other dogs apart from the Great Dane, which it equals in height. Its ancestors are thought to have been greyhound-type dogs that were brought to Ireland from the Middle East thousands of years ago, where they were crossed with mastiffs.

By the 15th century, these powerful dogs had become specialists in hunting wolves, which threatened Irish farmers and their animals. When the wolves were driven to extinction in the 1700s, the wolfhounds also started to die out until they were rescued by an army captain called George Graham. Despite their ferocious past, wolfhounds are the gentlest of giants. They are still capable of incredible strength and speed, but their favourite place to be is lounging on a rug (you'll need a big one!) at your feet.

POOCH PROFILE:
Country: Ireland **Size:** Giant; 71–86 cm (28–34 in) tall **Coat:** Rough, wiry fur; can be grey, brindle, black, cream and red **Personality:** Gentle, calm, noble

Strong jaws

Small, velvety ears

Long, muscular neck

Scruffy coat

Very deep chest

Large, round feet

Long, curved tail

IRISH SETTER

Setters are a type of dog used by hunters to find birds. When a setter locates a bird, they stand very still then lie down (this is called 'setting') to tell their human where the prey is. There are several breeds of setter – from the elegant English setter (p68) to Scotland's handsome Gordon setter. The chestnut-coated Irish setter is the most glamorous of the bunch.

But be warned! Beneath those glossy locks is a headstrong pooch with a rascally side that can get it into mischief. Made to move at top speed across the open countryside of their home country, they also have a lot of energy to burn. Keep an Irish setter busy with plenty of games of fetch and you have a fun-loving friend that will dazzle wherever it goes.

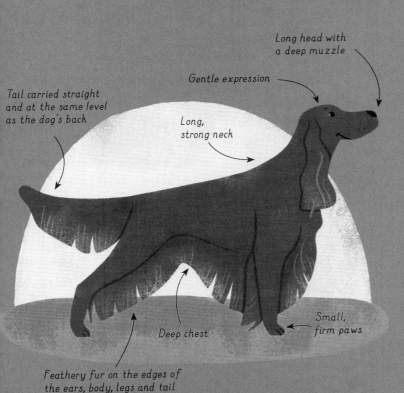

Long head with a deep muzzle

Gentle expression

Long, strong neck

Tail carried straight and at the same level as the dog's back

Deep chest

Small, firm paws

Feathery fur on the edges of the ears, body, legs and tail

POOCH PROFILE:
Country: Ireland **Size:** Large; 61–69 cm (24–27 in) tall **Coat:** Long and glossy; deep red in colour **Personality:** Affectionate, energetic, enthusiastic

SUPER HOUNDS

All dogs have incredible senses, but hounds take things to the next level. They are normally split into two groups – scenthounds, such as Basset hounds (p49) and coonhounds (p21), which follow their nose to find prey, and sighthounds, such as salukis (p82) and greyhounds (p41), which use their eyes to spot their target. While scenthounds are built for tracking a smell over long distances, sighthounds are made for sprinting and are some of the speediest dogs on the planet.

01 GRAND BLEU DE GASCOGNE (France)

Size: Large; 60–70 cm (23–27 in) tall
No one's quite sure when this handsome hound arrived on the scene, but it was used to track wolves in France as early as the 11th century. With calm tempers and distinguished grey-blue flecked coats, these dogs have a noble air. In 1785, a pack of Grand Bleus were gifted to the American politician (later President of the United States) George Washington, who compared their majestic howls to the sound of bells.

02 BEAGLE (UK)

Size: Small–Medium; 33–40 cm (13–16 in)
These small scenthounds were developed in Britain in the 1500s, where they were used to sniff out rabbits and hares. With gentle eyes, floppy ears and sweet, cheeky personalities, beagles are an adorable breed. But they can be stubborn! Once a beagle has got the smell of something tempting – whether that's a tasty treat or something stinky in a bin – there's no stopping them from nosing it out.

03 BLOODHOUND (Belgium/UK)

Size: Large; 58–69 cm (23–27 in) tall
A bloodhound is top dog when it comes to smelling-power. This floppy faced hound has an astounding 300 million scent cells in its nose – compared to a human's puny 5 million! Originally used to hunt deer in Belgium and Britain during the 1300s, today's bloodhounds make the ultimate detective dog, using their powerful noses to help police track down people who are lost or on the run.

A sighthound's eyes are set wide apart on its long, thin head. This gives the dog an incredible 270-degree field of vision, allowing it to spot prey behind it as well as nearly 1 km (half a mile) in front.

04 WHIPPET (UK)

Size: Medium; 44–51 cm (17–20 in) tall
Like a greyhound in miniature, the whippet is an elegant and gentle dog. The breed is thought to have been created in the 1800s by miners in northern England, who crossed greyhounds with terriers. Back then, these small, swift sighthounds were used to catch rabbits and rats, and to race. Nowadays, they make adaptable, sweet-natured pets that are as happy living in the city as the country.

05 PORTUGUESE PODENGO (Portugal)

Size: Small is 20–30 cm (8–12 in) tall; Medium is 40–54 cm (16–21 in) tall; Large is 55–70 cm (22–28 in) tall
These clever, lively hounds come in three sizes and can have either smooth or scruffy fur. They were developed in 16th-century Portugal to hunt a variety of wild animals – the larger dogs usually hunted deer, while the smaller dogs hunted rabbits. They are one of several Mediterranean hound breeds that use a triple-whammy of speed, sight and smell to catch their prey.

06 CIRNECO DELL'ETNA (Italy)

Size: Medium; 44–50 cm (17–19 in) tall
Dogs similar to the Cirneco dell'Etna (you say it 'cheer-nay-ko dell et-nuh') have been racing around the Italian island of Sicily for thousands of years and can be found on Sicilian coins dating from 500 BCE. As well as being quick on its feet, a Cirneco uses its keen sense of smell and enormous, pointy ears to track down rabbits. Named after the island's famous volcano, Mount Etna, these nimble hounds have fiery-coloured fur and an independent nature.

As well as a super-sensitive nose, scenthounds usually have floppy ears and baggy lips to help them get the most out of a smell. Their ears fan the smell up to their noses and their lips trap the smell near their nose.

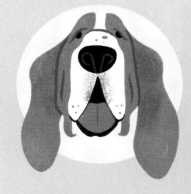

FRENCH BULLDOG

These sturdy French dogs have taken the world by storm in recent years. The breed is thought to have its roots in small English bulldogs, which were popular in the city of Nottingham, UK, in the 19th century. A group of lacemakers from the city moved to northern France and took their dogs with them. There, the bulldogs were crossed with other breeds, possibly pugs and terriers, to create the fully-fledged Frenchie – with its signature bat-like ears.

In time, French bulldogs became a popular sight in the bars and cafes of Paris, where they charmed artists and entertainers with their affectionate natures and goofy characters. Adaptable and easy-going, these sweethearts are still a favourite breed for city dwellers.

POOCH PROFILE:
Country: France **Size:** Small; 28–33 cm (11–13 in) tall
Coat: Short, smooth fur; various colours, including brindle, fawn and white with patches **Personality:** Playful, sweet, adaptable

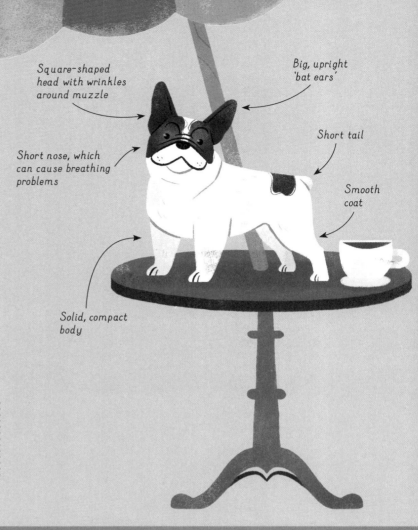

Square-shaped head with wrinkles around muzzle

Big, upright 'bat ears'

Short nose, which can cause breathing problems

Short tail

Smooth coat

Solid, compact body

Very large, feathery ears

Fine, delicate features and alert expression

Flowing coat

Long tail which curls over the dog's back in a plume

Neat, fairly long feet

PAPILLON

Favourite lapdogs of the famous 18th-century French queen, Marie Antoinette, these delicate dogs get their name from their sticky-up ears which look like the fluttery wings of the butterfly ('papillon' means 'butterfly' in French). Pups born in the same litter but with droopy ears are named 'phalene', which means 'moth'.

They may be dainty, but these dogs are tougher than they look, and they're smart, too. Their pretty locks need a lot of care and brushing, but papillons will equally enjoy showing off their stamina in activities such as agility.

POOCH PROFILE:
Country: France **Size:** Small; 20–28 cm (8–11 in) tall **Coat:** Long, fine hair; white with patches of various colours, including black, red or tricolour **Personality:** Elegant, intelligent, nimble

POODLE

The national dog of France, there is no sight more Parisian than that of a perfectly permed poodle trotting down a boulevard. Despite their French connections, these dogs are thought to have started out as duck retrievers in Germany. Their name comes from an old German word meaning 'to splash', which poodles today still love to do.

A poodle's floofy coat is often cut in a style that dates back to the dogs' retrieving days. Hunters clipped most of the poodle's hair short to help it move quickly through the water, but they left patches on the chest, tip of the tail and joints to protect the dog from the cold.

Long nose, with well-defined head

Very bright, intelligent eyes

Thick, curly hair (not fur) that keeps growing, so requires regular grooming

Deep chest

Straight front legs

POOCH PROFILE:
Country: France/Germany **Size:** Toy is under 28 cm (11 in) tall; Miniature is 28–38 cm (11–15 in) tall; Standard is more than 38 cm (15 in) tall **Coat:** Dense and curly; various colours, including black, white, apricot and grey **Personality:** Happy, lively, super-smart

As brainy as they are beautiful, poodles make outstanding assistance, therapy and guide dogs. And if you don't have room for a giant canine Einstein, the good news is that poodles also come in miniature and toy varieties.

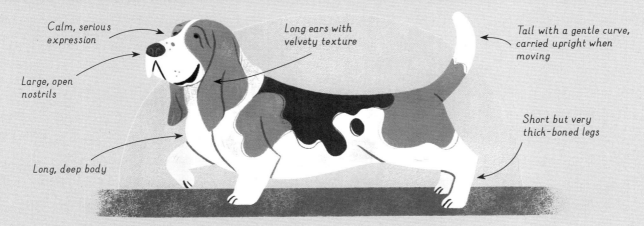

Calm, serious expression

Long ears with velvety texture

Tail with a gentle curve, carried upright when moving

Large, open nostrils

Short but very thick-boned legs

Long, deep body

BASSET HOUND

No dog has ears quite as floppy or eyes quite as soulful as the basset hound. Originally bred by medieval monks in France, the basset's short legs and long body allowed it to follow a scent through dense thickets, where taller hounds couldn't go. Its thick, baggy skin protected the dog from brambles, while its long ears would help sweep the smell up to its extremely powerful nose – only the bloodhound's nose is thought to be more sensitive.

On walks, bassets will follow their nose wherever it takes them, but they are extremely good-natured and lazy around the house. Those big, sad eyes mean they are experts at persuading you to part with treats. Just make sure they have a healthy balance of food and exercise, as bassets can have back and leg problems if they get too tubby.

POOCH PROFILE:
Country: France **Size:** Medium; 33–38 cm (13–15 in) tall **Coat:** Short, dense fur; usually tricolour or white and brown **Personality:** Loyal, gentle, stubborn

BELGIAN SHEPHERD DOGS

For centuries, Belgian farmers used these dogs to herd their sheep and guard their farms. The appearance of the dogs varied greatly in different parts of the country. Today, there are four different types, named after the areas where they were discovered. All share the same urge to work and eagerness to please.

The Malinois (you say it 'Mal-in-wah') is the smooth-coated variety. At first glance, they look like slender German shepherd dogs (p53). Their courageousness and trainability make them excellent police, search-and-rescue, and military dogs. To date, five Malinois have received the Dickin Medal – the highest military award any animal can receive – for their bravery.

Triangular, upright ears

Keen, intelligent expression

Firm mouth

Powerful but graceful body

Skull and muzzle roughly the same length

Long tail with a slight curve at the end

Long, strong legs

The three other Belgian shepherds are called the Tervueren, which has a long red, fawn or grey coat; the Groenendael, which has a long, black coat; and the Laekenois, which has a dense, wiry coat and is the rarest of the four. As well as herding, one of the Laekenois' original jobs was to guard a material called linen when it was put out to dry in the fields.

POOCH PROFILE:
Country: Belgium **Size:** Large; 56–66 cm (22–26 in) tall **Coat:** Three different coat types (long-haired, smooth-coated, wiry); various colours which relate to the coat type **Personality:** Hard-working, bright, loyal

BERNESE MOUNTAIN DOG

These mighty mountain dogs come from the farmlands of Switzerland. There they were used for centuries to guard homes, herd sheep and cattle, and pull carts of cheese, milk and crops to market. The breed almost went extinct in the 1880s, when the invention of tractors and cars put the dogs out of work. But they were saved by Swiss breeders and have gone on to become adored family companions.

With their distinct tricolour markings and long, glossy coat, Bernese mountain dogs are handsome pooches. Their good-looks are matched with an equally wonderful nature. Calm yet outgoing, playful yet patient, they make fantastic pets that are particularly gentle with kids. However, due to their size and mountaineering background, they need a good deal of space to romp about.

Cheerful expression

Flat, triangular-shaped ears

Bushy tail

Strong, flat skull

Round, sturdy feet

Soft, slightly wavy coat

Strong, muscly legs

POOCH PROFILE:
Country: Switzerland **Size:** Large; 58–70 cm (23–27 in) tall **Coat:** Long, silky fur; jet-black body with red on chest, cheeks, eyes and legs, and a symmetrical white marking on head and chest **Personality:** Strong, devoted, good-natured

Fluffy tail that curls over the dog's back

Small, upright ears with velvety texture

'Spectacle' markings around eyes

Fox-like face

Compact feet for jumping on and off boats

Short body

Dense ruff of fur around neck

KEESHOND

This silver-coated spitz made its name as a watchdog on Dutch canal boats in the 18th century and is now the Netherlands' national dog. Built for a life on the waterways, the keeshond ('kayz-hawnd') is a compact dog that is perfectly happy to get its nimble paws wet.

Perhaps because their ancestors lived in such close quarters with people, keeshonds love to be near you and rarely let their favourite person out of their sight. They are loud barkers that keep a watchful eye on your front door, but they are usually friendly towards everyone who comes through it. A combination of light-coloured fur and dark lines round their eyes make these pooches look like they're wearing glasses, giving them a professor-ish expression.

POOCH PROFILE:
Country: Netherlands **Size:** Medium; 43–46 cm (17–18 in) tall **Coat:** Dense, thick fur; a mix of grey and black **Personality:** Friendly, confident, alert

SCHNAUZERS

The schnauzer family is made up of three different-sized breeds – miniature, standard and giant. Each one sports the bushy beard and seriously shaggy eyebrows that give the dog its name – 'schnauzer' means 'whiskered snout' in German. The standard is the original breed, which started out as a farm dog during the Middle Ages. They soon showed they could take on a variety of farmyard tasks, leading to the creation of the three specialist sizes. The mini dogs were used to catch rats, the standard for pulling small carts and the giant for herding cattle.

POOCH PROFILE:
Country: Germany **Size:** Miniature is 33–36 cm (13–14 in) tall; Standard is 45–48 cm (18–19 in) tall; Giant is 60–70 cm (23–27 in) tall **Coat:** Dense, wiry; black, pepper and salt, silver **Personality:** Active, sociable, fearless

DACHSHUND

With its unmistakable shape and chirpy character, the dachshund is one of the world's most popular pups. They were first bred to find badgers in twisty underground burrows ('dachshund' means 'badger dog' in German), a task that their sausage-shaped bodies and stubby legs are perfectly designed for. Today, you're just as likely to see a dachshund wiggling its way under a duvet as diving down a burrow. They make lovable pets, and will guard your front door with a surprisingly loud, big-dog bark.

POOCH PROFILE:
Country: Germany **Size:** Miniature is 13–15 cm (5–6 in) tall; Standard is 20–23 cm (8–9 in) tall **Coat:** Smooth, wire-haired or long-haired; colours include black and tan, red, black and chocolate **Personality:** Brave, playful, strong-minded

WEIMARANER

This refined breed was created in the 1800s by a duke who wanted a hunting dog fit for his grand estate near the city of Weimar in Germany. He is thought to have crossed bloodhounds with pointers and other European hounds to create these show-stopping canines with stunning silver coats. For the next hundred years, Weimaraners ('vy-mah-rah-ners') were prized by German aristocrats, so much so that only an elite circle was allowed to own them.

POOCH PROFILE:
Country: Germany **Size:** Large; 56–69 cm (22–27 in) tall **Coat:** Usually short and sleek, though a rare long-haired variety also exists; silver-grey **Personality:** Faithful, obedient, energetic

BOXER

The boxer was created in the 1800s by crossing an old German breed called the bullenbeisser (meaning 'bull biter') with British bulldogs. How the breed got their English name is less certain, but it may have come from the way the dogs 'box' with their front paws when they play. Boxers have taken on various jobs over the years – from carrying messages for troops in both world wars to working as police dogs. Combining courage, cleverness and a slightly goofy side, they make fun-loving companions that are especially gentle with children.

POOCH PROFILE:

Country: Germany **Size:** Large; 53–63 cm (21–25 in) tall **Coat:** Short and glossy; fawn or brindle
Personality: Bright, confident, family-orientated

ROTTWEILER

The roots of the Rottweiler reach back to ancient times, when Romans marching across Europe took cattle with them to feed their troops and mastiff-type dogs to keep the cows in check. Some of these dogs found themselves in the town of Rottweil in south-west Germany, where they were adopted by local farmers. Crossed with sheepdogs, the Roman dogs were developed into a breed that had the intelligence and strength to guide cows to market and the courage to guard the herd from robbers on the road. Sadly, the Rottweiler's protective temperament and powerful size has given them a bad reputation but with the right training, a Rottie can make a gentle, affectionate pet for a kind and sensible owner.

POOCH PROFILE:

Country: Germany **Size:** Large; 58–69 cm (23–27 in)
Coat: Usually coarse or flat; black and tan markings
Personality: Brave, intelligent, biddable

GERMAN SHEPHERD

In the late 1800s, a German military captain called Max von Stephanitz set about creating a herding dog that was the best of the best. In doing so, he made a pooch that can turn its paw to pretty much any task. Intelligent and keen to learn, German shepherds do an astounding variety of jobs – from being the first breed used as guide dogs for blind people to acting as police and search-and-rescue dogs. German shepherds are high-energy and need to be kept busy with physical and mental activities. If they can seem a little aloof with strangers that's because they focus their abundant energy, loyalty and love on their family.

POOCH PROFILE:

Country: Germany **Size:** Large; 58–63 cm (23–25 in) tall **Coat:** Short or long; black muzzle and back with gold and grey fur **Personality:** Smart, brave, devoted

TERRIFIC TERRIERS

Most of the world's terriers have their origins in the UK or Ireland, where they were used to catch rodents and other wild creatures. Terriers are tough and fairly small dogs, but what they lack in size they make up for in personality ... BIG time! A typical terrier is clever and comical, fearless and feisty. They may not get on with every dog in the park, but no day is ever dull with these plucky pooches by your side.

JACK RUSSELL (UK)

Size: Small; 25–30 cm (10–12 in) tall
The look and shape of one Jack Russell can vary greatly to another. The ancestors of these sparky terriers were bred by an English vicar called John 'Jack' Russell, who wanted an energetic dog to accompany him on fox hunts. Jack Russells have minds (and voices!) of their own, but with clear training make cheerful, cheeky companions.

IRISH TERRIER (Ireland)

Size: Medium; 46–48 cm (18–19 in) tall
This dashing terrier has a daredevil character to match its flame-red fur. Originally used as watchdogs and rat-catchers on Irish farms, these dogs are bold, full of life and always on the alert. They love being around people and make great playmates. Early Irish terriers came in various colours, but today, they are best known for their red coats.

WEST HIGHLAND WHITE TERRIER (UK)

Size: Small; 28 cm (11 in) tall
These smart, spirited little dogs were developed in Scotland during the 19th century to catch rats. They share the same family tree as the Scottish terrier (p44) and other Scottish breeds such as the Cairn terrier. Their fun-loving personalities make West Highland white terriers (or 'Westies') popular family pets, who lap up attention and never fail to let you know that the postman's at the door.

BEDLINGTON TERRIER (UK)

Size: Medium; 41 cm (16 in) tall
With a woolly coat, tasselled ears and whippy tail, the Bedlington terrier is a dog that turns heads. Despite their lamb-like looks, these clever and quick dogs were originally bred to catch rodents and rabbits in north-east England during the 1800s. Milder than most terriers, today's Bedlingtons make sweet, cuddly companions, who live for frolics in the park.

AIREDALE TERRIER (UK)

Size: Large; 56–61 cm (22–24 in) tall
Nicknamed the 'King of the Terriers', the Airedale is the largest terrier breed. Originally created in Yorkshire in the 1800s by crossing hounds with terriers, these super-sized rat-catchers were used as farm dogs as well as for hunting. Strong and courageous, Airedales also carried messages and medical supplies to British troops in the trenches during World War I.

STAFFORDSHIRE BULL TERRIER (UK)

Size: Medium; 36–41 cm (14–16 in) tall
Staffordshire bull terriers were created in the city of Birmingham, UK, in the 1800s by crossing bulldogs (p41) with terriers. These solid pooches were originally used as fighting dogs and this history gave the breed a bad name for many years. Underneath all the muscle is a sweet-natured softie that is guaranteed to greet you with a wiggly bum and a smile as big as its generous heart.

EUROPE (South/East)

From the spindly Ibizan hound to the mop-like Hungarian puli, the dogs of southern and eastern Europe are a unique and fascinating pack. These are dogs whose ancestors may have sailed to Europe's shores on the ships of ancient traders, sat on the laps of Roman emperors or guarded flocks from ravenous wolves on remote mountain farms. Some, like the Dalmatian, are known the world over, while others, like the Lagotto Romagnolo, are only just starting to venture beyond their home country.

ESTRELA MOUNTAIN DOG
PORTUGAL

CATALAN SHEEPDOG
SPAIN

PORTUGUESE WATER DOG
PORTUGAL

IBIZAN HOUND
SPAIN

CESKY TERRIER
CZECH REPUBLIC

The whiskered faces of Cesky terriers have appeared on postage stamps in their home country of the Czech Republic.

POLISH LOWLAND SHEEPDOG
POLAND

HUNGARIAN PULI
HUNGARY

BERGAMASCO SHEEPDOG
ITALY

HUNGARIAN VIZSLA
HUNGARY

DALMATIAN
CROATIA OR MEDITERRANEAN REGION

Like human fingerprints, the spots on a Dalmatian are unique to the dog. Dalmatians even have spots in their mouths and on their paw pads!

ITALIAN SPINONE
ITALY

LAGOTTO ROMAGNOLO
ITALY

ITALIAN GREYHOUND
ITALY

Italian greyhounds can count royalty among their many fans. Catherine the Great of Russia and Queen Victoria of Britain are just two monarchs known to have owned them.

MALTESE
UNKNOWN

In medieval times, wealthy people kept Maltese dogs beside their bed at night to draw away the fleas!

PHARAOH HOUND
MALTA

CATALAN SHEEPDOG

This energetic sheepdog comes from Catalonia, in north-eastern Spain. Although its exact origins are lost in the mists of time, the breed is thought to have its roots in herding dogs introduced to the country by the ancient Romans.

Catalan sheepdogs became a firm favourite among medieval farmers and can still be found rounding up flocks in the Pyrenees mountains. However, they are not as numerous as they once were. In the 1960s, the breed faced extinction as many Catalonian shepherds sold their farms and moved to the cities. Fans of the breed saved the remaining dogs and established a breeding programme, but they remain rare. If you're lucky enough to meet a Catalan sheepdog, you'll discover a dependable pooch, with one of the most adorably scruffy-looking faces around.

Flat or slightly wavy coat with a rough texture

Triangular ears

Tail curved at tip, held upright when active

Prominent moustache, beard and eyebrows

Strong, muscular body

Double dewclaws, firm feet and paw pads

These courageous canines were used as messenger dogs during the Spanish Civil War and World War II.

POOCH PROFILE:
Country: Spain **Size:** Medium–Large; 45–55 cm (17–21 in) tall **Coat:** Medium-length; black, fawn, sable or grey **Personality:** Attentive, cheerful, loyal

---

Pink nose

Large, upright ears

Very lean body

Thin tail

Fine, long face

Smooth or rough-haired coat

IBIZAN HOUND

This big-eared hound is an ancient breed, believed to be descended from dogs whose portraits decorate the walls of Egyptian tombs. About 3,000 years ago, its ancestors were brought to the Spanish island of Ibiza, where the breed was developed into a top-notch rabbit hunter.

Not only are these dogs lightning-quick, but they can also leap almost 2 m (6 ft) from a standing position – so they need a secure garden to keep them safe. Owners of Ibizans should keep an eye on what they leave out in the kitchen. An Ibizan hound isn't a greedy dog, but it will happily help itself to any unattended snacks thanks to its height and jumping skills. Although they have a cheeky side, these dogs make gentle-natured pets.

POOCH PROFILE:
Country: Spain **Size:** Large; 56–74 cm (22–29 in) tall **Coat:** Smooth or rough; white, fawn or red, or mix of these **Personality:** Quiet, agile, elegant

PORTUGUESE WATER DOG

You can think of Portuguese water dogs (or 'Porties') as the sheepdogs of the sea. These cheerful, water-loving pooches were first developed by fishermen along Portugal's coast to herd shoals of fish into waiting nets. They also helped out with other ocean-based tasks, such as retrieving lost gear from the waves and carrying messages between boats.

The number of Porties declined at the start of the 20th century, when fishing methods changed and modernized. In 2009, the breed was given a boost after a Portie puppy called Bo was adopted by President Barack Obama and his family and became the 'First Dog of the United States'.

Traditional 'lion cut' hairdo

Curled tail, often trimmed with a tuft at the tip

Generous coat, either tightly curled or loosely waved

Strong, muscly legs

Round, flat, webbed feet

In a Portie's traditional 'lion trim', the hair on the front half of the dog is left to grow long and the back end is shaved short. This cut had a practical purpose, giving the dog some protection from the chilly waters of the Atlantic Ocean while allowing its legs and rudder-like tail to cut through the waves.

POOCH PROFILE:
Country: Portugal **Size:** Medium–Large; 43–57 cm (17–22 in) tall **Coat:** Curly or wavy; usually black or brown, or black or brown with white markings **Personality:** Playful, affectionate, energetic

ESTRELA MOUNTAIN DOG

With fur the colour of a dusty Portuguese plain, Estrela ('es-treh-lah') mountain dogs are one of the country's oldest breeds and are named for its highest mountain range. These dogs were built for tough work, guiding their flocks across rugged peaks and lowlands by day and guarding the sheep from wolves by night.

An Estrela will take its role as a guardian of your home very seriously, but behind that muscle, fluff and booming bark is a kind dog that is immensely loving and loyal towards its family. Estrelas need a decent-sized garden to call their own, as they remain mountaineers at heart.

Black fur on face

Small ears that fold backwards

Calm expression

Males have a thick mane of hair around their necks.

Fairly short back

Tail hooked at the tip

POOCH PROFILE:
Country: Portugal **Size:** Giant; 62–72 cm (24–28 in) tall **Coat:** Short- or long-haired; fawn with reddish brown highlights, grey or brindle **Personality:** Faithful, intelligent, hardy

DOGS WITH JOBS

Dogs have been lending a paw to humans for thousands of years – from herding and hunting to providing companionship and protection. In more recent times, many dogs have put the skills perfected by their ancestors to use in some incredible ways.

SUPER SHEEPDOGS

Old English sheepdogs, Hungarian pulis and Australian cattle dogs are some of the many breeds traditionally used to help round up farm animals. But no dog can guide a flock with quite as much style and skill as a border collie.

Originally bred to herd sheep in the hilly borderlands between England, Scotland and Wales, border collies are some of the quickest, smartest and most hard-working dogs on the planet. They have a famously intense stare, which they use to intimidate sheep in the field, an uncanny ability to anticipate commands, and a tremendous desire to work. Even a pet collie will attempt to round up almost anything that moves – whether that's tennis balls, other dogs or you!

HELPFUL HOUNDS

Canines that provide special support and companionship to people are called assistance dogs. Some help blind, deaf or disabled people to get around safely. Others are trained to alert humans to medical conditions, such as seizures. Therapy dogs provide comfort and emotional support to people – such as someone with a long-term illness.

Labradors and golden retrievers are some of the most popular guide dogs – they are loyal, smart and large enough to provide physical support for the person walking alongside them. Smaller breeds, such as miniature poodles and cockapoos, are often used as hearing dogs. They are clever and friendly, and their portable size means they can easily accompany their owner to lots of different places.

COURAGEOUS CANINES

Police dogs do all kinds of difficult and dangerous jobs. Belgian Malinois and German shepherds are often used to catch criminals. Originally bred to round up sheep, they are fast and strong enough to tackle a person to the ground, but clever enough to know when someone isn't a threat.

These breeds also make excellent search-and-rescue ('SAR') dogs, helping to find people who are lost or injured. Border collies and Labradors are popular SAR breeds, too, due to their eagerness to learn and devotion to people. Meanwhile, breeds with super-sensitive noses, such as bloodhounds and springer spaniels, make top-class sniffer dogs, tracking down items such as drugs or explosives and keeping people safe.

FURRY FILM STARS

Dogs of all shapes and sizes have been stealing scenes in the movies since the earliest days of cinema. Two of the most famous dog actors in history are Terry, a Cairn terrier who shot to fame as Toto in *The Wizard of Oz*, and Pal, a rough collie who created the role of Lassie for film and TV.

Canine actors are highly trained dogs that are usually taught from puppyhood to respond to hand signals and commands … and, of course, are rewarded with lots of treats! Several dogs are often used to play one role in a film. A dog that is great at jumping will be used for action scenes, while a dog that is good at paw tricks will be used for close-up shots.

Tennis Champs

In 2016 and 2017, at a tennis tournament in Brazil, South America, rescue dogs were trained to fetch balls on the court. The scheme promoted the work of local rescue centres and encouraged people to adopt homeless dogs.

Pest Controller

Since 2018, a Weimaraner called Riley has been on a mission to sniff out pests in the Museum of Fine Arts in Boston, USA. Riley alerts his human colleagues to the presence of insects that can harm paintings, helping staff to preserve the precious art collection.

Wildlife Rescuer

A beagle called Captain Ron has been using his super nose to find the eggs of endangered sea turtles in Florida, USA. Ron's work allows conservationists to monitor the eggs and keep them from being disturbed by predators or other people on the beach.

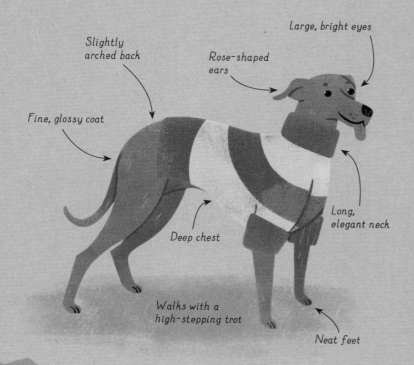

Slightly arched back

Large, bright eyes

Rose-shaped ears

Fine, glossy coat

Deep chest

Long, elegant neck

Walks with a high-stepping trot

Neat feet

ITALIAN GREYHOUND

This elegant dog has the swiftness of a full-sized greyhound (p41) mixed with the sweet, doting nature of a lapdog. Italian greyhounds have been snuggling up to people since the time of the Roman Empire but the breed was given a massive boost in the Middle Ages, when they popped up in portraits of wealthy merchants and royalty.

A true greyhound in miniature, these little dogs will gamely dart after small furry animals in the park and love to have a good zoom about. But they can be fussy. An Italian greyhound will look bewildered if you suggest a walk in the rain and will be glad of a woolly jumper in cold weather.

POOCH PROFILE:
Country: Italy **Size:** Small; 32–38 cm (12–15 in) tall
Coat: Short, fine fur; comes in various colours, including black, cream, red and white with markings
Personality: Nimble, affectionate, sensitive

BERGAMASCO SHEEPDOG

The Bergamasco ('buh-guh-ma-skow') sheepdog takes a shaggy coat to another level! Although this dog's head-turning hair looks high-maintenance, a Bergamasco doesn't need to be brushed, doesn't shed and is practically self-cleaning – just a few baths a year will do.

Bergamasco puppies are born with fluffy coats, which become rougher and develop naturally into thick, flat mats called 'flocks' as the dogs reach adulthood. These flocks protect the dogs from the extreme weather conditions in the Italian Alps, where Bergamascos have herded and guarded sheep for centuries. As well as keeping it warm and dry in the winter, a Bergamasco's coat helps to control the dog's body temperature in summer, allowing air to flow between the flocks and down to the dog's skin. The mats provide protection from the sun's rays and insect bites, too.

Calm, caring and clever, these scruffy sheepdogs will happily welcome kids as well as other animals into their family herd.

Strong and muscly bodies underneath fur

Thick coat that keeps the dog cool in hot weather and warm in cold weather

Slightly curved tail, waved like a flag when excited

Hard paw pads

A lot of hair, which grows in thick clumps

POOCH PROFILE:
Country: Italy **Size:** Large; 54–62 cm (21–24 in) tall
Coat: Long and matted; various shades of grey and black, fawn and isabella (pale grey-brown) **Personality:** Intelligent, protective, patient

ITALIAN SPINONE

Rough-haired dogs similar to the grizzly spinone ('spin-o-nay') have been by the side of Italian huntsmen since the 1400s. Used to find and retrieve birds in the mountains and marshlands of north-west Italy, these dogs are strong, tough and built for stamina rather than speed. Their name is thought to refer to the prickly undergrowth that the dogs were bred to barge through during a hunt ('spina' means 'thorn' in Italian). Or it could relate to the spiky texture of the dogs' coats themselves, which, along with their thick skin, provided protection from thorns.

Spinones' kind, gentle nature and adorable, gruff looks have won them fans both in and outside their home country. They need long walks and room to roam about, but make brilliant companions for outdoorsy families.

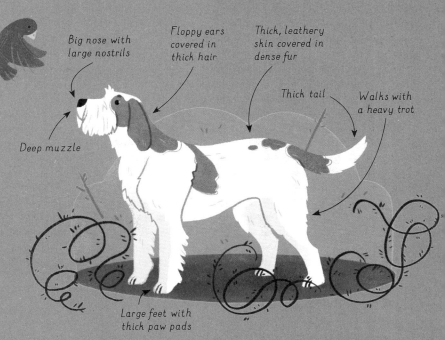

Big nose with large nostrils

Floppy ears covered in thick hair

Thick, leathery skin covered in dense fur

Thick tail

Walks with a heavy trot

Deep muzzle

Large feet with thick paw pads

POOCH PROFILE:
Country: Italy **Size:** Large; 58–70 cm (22–27 in) tall
Coat: Thick, coarse fur; colours include white, white and orange, and white and brown **Personality:** Patient, friendly, gentle

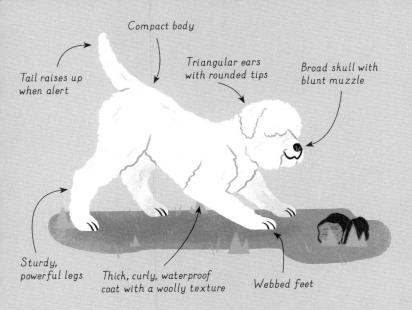

Compact body

Triangular ears with rounded tips

Broad skull with blunt muzzle

Tail raises up when alert

Sturdy, powerful legs

Thick, curly, waterproof coat with a woolly texture

Webbed feet

POOCH PROFILE:
Country: Italy **Size:** Medium; 41–48 cm (16–19 in) tall
Coat: Thick coat made of ring-shaped curls; colours include white, white with brown, brown, and orange with white markings **Personality:** Loving, eager, clever

LAGOTTO ROMAGNOLO

The teddy-bearish Lagotto Romagnolo ('lah-go-toe ro-man-yo-lo') is a dog of many talents. They originally came from a region of lakes and marshes in north-eastern Italy ('lago' means 'lake' in Italian), where they were used by hunters to retrieve ducks from the water. Many of these marshes were drained in the early 20th century and the Lagotto's work dried up. But their super-sensitive noses led to a new job – sniffing and digging out truffles, a rare and extremely expensive type of fungus.

Affectionate and sweet-natured, Lagottos are adored in their home country and are becoming popular pets outside of Italy, too. Although these dogs like an active lifestyle, they will happily chill out with you after a good run (or, better yet, a swim!). Their beautiful curly coats, however, grow quickly and require quite a bit of maintenance to keep them looking smart.

DALMATIAN

Peppered in brilliant black or brown spots, the Dalmatian is one of the most distinctive breeds on the planet. However, the origins of these dogs are far from clear. Long before they were outsmarting Cruella de Vil in *One Hundred and One Dalmatians*, these spotty dogs were companions of the nomadic Romani people. For a time, they were also used as hunting dogs along Croatia's Dalmatian coast.

Croatia may have given the dogs their name, but the breed was properly developed in Britain in the 1800s as a coach dog. Groups of Dalmatians would run beside a horse-drawn carriage to keep the horses under control and guard from highwaymen. When these dogs reached the USA, they were trained to run ahead of the horse teams that pulled fire trucks. To this day, Dalmatians are a popular firefighting mascot in America.

When Dalmatians are born, their fur is completely white. Their spots don't start to appear until the dog is a few weeks old and get stronger as it grows up.

The colour of a Dalmatian's nose and toenails always matches the colour of its spots.

Flat skull

Elegant neck

Deep chest to hold large lungs and heart

Round, clear spots – lots of them!

Muscular legs

Slightly curved tail

Round, firm feet

Unsurprisingly, these dashing dogs love to run ... and run and run! Dalmatians are rarely ever still and can be a bit of a handful if their energy isn't channelled into long walks or agility games. But if you can match their fast-paced lifestyle, Dalmatians make firm friends and the most stylish jogging buddies around.

POOCH PROFILE:

Country: Unknown – likely Croatia or Mediterranean region **Size:** Large; 56–61 cm (22–23 in) tall
Coat: Short, dense and glossy; pure white with either black or brown ('liver') spots **Personality:** Outgoing, friendly, energetic

MALTESE

Although they are named after Malta, an island in the Mediterranean Sea, it's not known where these little white dogs came from originally. One thing's for certain – they have been pampered across Europe for millennia. They've popped up in the writings of ancient Greek philosophers and sat on the laps of Roman emperors.

While Maltese are sweet-tempered dogs that adore the company of people, they are feisty canines at heart and will be just as enthusiastic about guarding your front door as getting cuddles. Maltese make brilliant students for doggie agility classes, but they really come into their own when they're on the go. Watch one of these dogs trot round a room and it almost seems to float across the floor, sweeping its fabulous hair behind it.

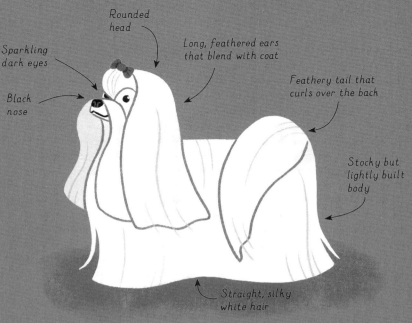

Rounded head

Sparkling dark eyes

Long, feathered ears that blend with coat

Black nose

Feathery tail that curls over the back

Stocky but lightly built body

Straight, silky white hair

POOCH PROFILE:

Country: Unknown – likely somewhere in southern Europe **Size:** Small; 25 cm (10 in) tall **Coat:** Long and straight; pure white **Personality:** Gentle, lively, intelligent

PHARAOH HOUND

The pharaoh hound sounds and looks like it would be at home sunning itself on the steps of an Egyptian pyramid, but the breed was actually developed on the island of Malta, where it's the national dog. Its ancestors certainly came from ancient Egypt and it shares the same roots as the Ibizan hound (p58) and the Cirneco dell'Etna (p47).

On Malta, these handsome hounds made their name as rabbit hunters, using their sharp eyes, strong nose and ginormous ears to track down their prey, and their long, strong legs when they needed a burst of speed. They're affectionate pets and can express their feelings in a way no other dog can – you can tell when a pharaoh hound is happy because its nose and ears blush pink!

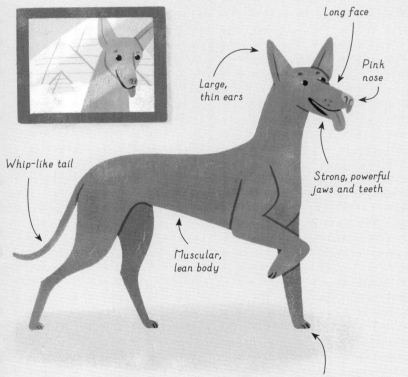

Long face

Pink nose

Large, thin ears

Whip-like tail

Strong, powerful jaws and teeth

Muscular, lean body

Firm, nimble feet

POOCH PROFILE:

Country: Malta **Size:** Large; 53–63 cm (21–25 in) tall **Coat:** Short and glossy; tan colour sometimes with white on the chest **Personality:** Friendly, alert, playful

POLISH LOWLAND SHEEPDOG

The shaggy-haired Polish lowland sheepdog, or 'PON', was bred to guard flocks on the rolling plains of central Poland. PONs have been in Poland since at least the 13th century and are thought to be descended from Asian shepherd dogs and possibly related to the Hungarian puli (see opposite).

These dogs are built for a tough, outdoor life. They have a double coat with a harsh topcoat to protect against all weathers and a fluffy undercoat to keep them toasty through bitterly cold winters. Through that bushy fuzz of hair peer alert eyes that sparkle with intelligence and a keen desire to work. A PON will look to you for instructions and is always ready to spring into action.

During World War II, a brave PON called Psyche lived in Warsaw, Poland's capital city. Psyche is said to have been able to tell when bombs were going to going to fall on the city and warned people so they could get to safety.

Broad head

Fur especially long on the dog's head

Rectangular-shaped body

Sometimes born without a tail

Tough paw pads

Lots and lots of hair that makes the dog seem bigger than it is

POOCH PROFILE:
Country: Poland **Size:** Medium; 42–50 cm (16–19 in) tall **Coat:** Long, thick coat; colours include black and white, brown and white, and grey **Personality:** Confident, active, bright

Coat clipped short on back and neck, left long on face, legs and tummy

Graceful and strong neck

Triangular ears that hang close to the dog's cheeks

Long head

Long tail

Slightly wavy fur

Medium-length body

Well-muscled legs

POOCH PROFILE:
Country: Czech Republic **Size:** Small; 25–32 cm (9–12 in) tall **Coat:** Wavy and silky; light brown or dark to silver-grey **Personality:** Cheerful, reserved, clever

CESKY TERRIER

The national dog of the Czech Republic, the Cesky terrier (you say it 'chess-key') is a rare and fairly recent breed. It was developed in the 1940s by a man called Frantisek Horak, who wanted to create a terrier that could hunt rats as well as any other terrier, but would be a little more chilled-out when off duty. He crossed Scottish terriers (p44) with a Welsh breed called the Sealyham terrier to make his dream doggo.

A Cesky's sleek coat is usually clipped short around the body and left long and wavy around the legs and head. This highlights the dog's most distinguishing features – its splendid beard and eyebrows. These gentlemanly dogs are always game for an adventure with their special humans, but they can be shy around people they don't know.

HUNGARIAN PULI

The one-of-a-kind Hungarian puli ('poo-lee') may look like a mop on legs, but beneath those locks is an acrobatic herding dog. Puli puppies are born with fuzzy fur that grows into thick cords as the dog matures. These cords keep the puli warm and dry, and jiggle about delightfully when the dog is on the move. And pulis move a lot! They are nimble dogs, bred to round up sheep. Working pulis sometimes even hop on to the backs of sheep to get a view of the herd.

Traditionally, pulis worked alongside another cord-coated breed called the komondor on Hungarian farms. Big enough to see off wolves and bears, the komondors guarded the flock at night, while the smaller pulis kept an eye on things during the day.

POOCH PROFILE:
Country: Hungary **Size:** Small–Medium; 37–44 cm (14–17 in) tall **Coat:** Long, naturally occurring cords; can be black, grey, fawn or white **Personality:** Clever, agile, energetic

Bright-red tongue

Lively expression

Tail curled tightly over back

Round feet with springy paw pads

Moves with quick, short steps

Whole body covered in long cords, including face and tail

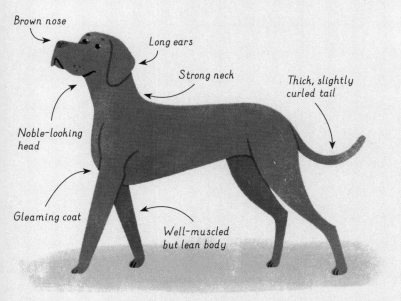

Brown nose

Long ears

Strong neck

Thick, slightly curled tail

Noble-looking head

Gleaming coat

Well-muscled but lean body

POOCH PROFILE:
Country: Hungary **Size:** Large; 53–64 cm (21–25 in) tall **Coat:** Short and smooth; russet-gold in colour **Personality:** Affectionate, lively, sensitive

HUNGARIAN VIZSLA

Vizslas are descended from hunting dogs that were brought to Hungary by the Magyar people, who settled in the region over 1,000 years ago. By the 1300s, these handsome dogs were prized by Hungarian noblemen as top-class pointers and retrievers.

A vizsla's russet-gold fur is very short, has no undercoat and feels slightly oily when you touch it. All of these features mean it's perfectly designed to keep the dog cool while searching for birds on the hot Hungarian plains.

Vizslas love exercise and the outdoors but more than anything else they love to be around people. A vizsla will stick by your side and, despite its size, probably attempt to sit on your lap if you'll let it.

FINDING AND FETCHING DOGS

Some of the best dogs to play a game of Frisbee with include pointers, setters, retrievers and water dogs. These are breeds that were originally created to help humans on hunts. Pointers were bred to be specialists at spotting prey – staring in the direction of their target with a paw raised and tail straight. A setter's method is similar, but it crouches low to the ground instead. Meanwhile, retrievers and water dogs were trained to be the best fetchers in the business. Let's meet a few!

01 GERMAN SHORTHAIRED POINTER (Germany)

Size: Large; 53–64 cm (21–25 in) tall
In the 1800s, German hunters crossed Spanish and English pointers to create this athletic and multi-talented pooch. With a strong nose for tracking, the perfect posture for pointing and a gentle mouth for retrieving, these dogs are game for pretty much any task. German shorthaired pointers need a good deal of exercise to stay trim and happy, but they're worth every mile.

02 ENGLISH SETTER (UK)

Size: Large; 61–69 cm (24–27 in) tall
Sporting a speckled coat, a proud head and some of the gentlest eyes in the canine kingdom, the English setter is a good-looking and sweet-tempered dog. They are often said to be the most easy-going members of the beautiful but boisterous setter family. That said, English setters are born to run and are happiest when they can feel the wind in their glossy fur and the open countryside beneath their paws.

03 BRACCO ITALIANO (Italy)

Size: Large; 55–67 cm (21–26 in) tall
With origins that stretch back to the 4th or 5th century BCE, Braccos are thought to be Europe's oldest breed of pointer. Originally, two distinct versions of the Bracco were developed in neighbouring regions of northern Italy – one to hunt in the mountains, the other to hunt in the marshy lowlands. These docile dogs have hound ancestors to thank for their noble noses and extremely soulful expressions.

🐾 04 KOOIKERHONDJE (Netherlands)

Size: Medium; 35–42 cm (14–16 in) tall

The kooikerhondje's ('coy-ker-hond-tsje') original job was to attract the attention of unsuspecting ducks by waving its feathery white tail in the air. Prized by Dutch hunters for centuries, these water dogs are keen, confident and fast on their feet. They also have a long association with royalty – legend has it that a loyal kooikerhonje saved the life of a Dutch prince by barking at would-be assassins.

🐾 05 FLAT-COATED RETRIEVER (UK)

Size: Large; 56–61 cm (22–24 in) tall

The beautiful flat-coated retriever was developed in the UK in the 1800s to collect ducks on hunts, and was the most popular retrieving breed, until the golden retriever and Labrador came along. The flat-coat is similar to a Labrador in size but has a more elegant build and a lush, feathery black or brown coat. These friendly dogs are outgoing and up for endless games of fetch.

🐾 06 BARBET (France)

Size: Medium; 53–65 cm (20–25 in) tall

A relative of the poodle, this woolly-coated water dog is named after its distinctive beard – 'barbe' means 'beard' in French. The barbet (pronounced 'bar-bay') loves nothing better than splashing around in muddy marshlands. It's done this for centuries in its home country, where it originally earned its keep as a duck retriever. Cheerful and tireless, they are a rare breed and not seen much outside of France.

SLOUGHI
ALGERIA, TUNISIA, MOROCCO, LIBYA

AZAWAKH
BURKINA FASO, MALI, NIGER

BASENJI
DEMOCRATIC REPUBLIC OF THE CONGO

AIDI
MOROCCO

The Azawakh was originally developed to be a guard dog as well as a hunter. Packs of Azawakh are still used by nomadic peoples across the Sahara to protect their camps from prowling predators, such as hyenas.

COTON DE TULEAR MADAGASCAR

Cotons are acrobatic dogs and have a habit of walking around on their back legs.

RHODESIAN RIDGEBACK ZIMBABWE

As well as hunting down lions, Rhodesian ridgebacks were originally used for a variety of jobs, including herding oxen, chasing baboons off farmland and guarding homes.

A basenji's voice box is shaped in an unusual way, which means the dog can't bark. Basenjis that are used for hunting in the thick forests of the Congo often have bells tied round their necks, so their humans can work out where they are.

AFRICA

If you like the idea of dogs that can stand up to lions, outrun gazelles and yodel their hearts out (that's right, yodel), then you've come to the right continent. Africa is a land of ancient and intriguing breeds. Long before most European dogs came on the scene, many of Africa's canines were cosying up to pharaohs or helping humans hunt and farm in some of the most challenging environments on Earth. Let's say hi!

Large, dark eyes with a wistful expression

Triangular ears

Long, graceful neck

Long, refined skull and muzzle

The name 'sloughi' comes from an Arabic word meaning 'sighthound'.

Short coat

Thin tail

Slim waist

Long, muscly legs built for short bursts of speed

SLOUGHI

The sloughi ('sloo-gi') is a lean, keen sighthound found across the desert landscapes of Algeria, Tunisia, Morocco and Libya. This ancient breed has been developed by the Berber people of the region for thousands of years. Its original job was to chase down fast-moving creatures, such as gazelles and jackals, and it is still used in its home lands as a hunter as well as a watchdog.

Sloughis have very fine, short coats and barely any fat on their bodies. This keeps the dogs cool in the desert and ensures they are light enough to sprint across the sands. Coats range from red and brindle to cream, but the most common is a light sandy colour with black fur on the dog's muzzle and around the eyes.

Although they are serious hunters, sloughis are gentle and affectionate with their family – less so with strangers, who they'll treat rather haughtily. Sloughis also love their creature comforts and won't hesitate to make a beeline for the cosiest bed in the house. If that happens to be yours, prepare to budge up!

POOCH PROFILE:

Country: Algeria, Tunisia, Morocco and Libya
Size: Large; 61–72 cm (24–28 in) tall **Coat:** Fine and short; sandy, red, brindle or black – sandy and brindle dogs often have black markings on their face
Personality: Quiet, elegant, fast

AIDI

The aidi (pronounced 'ah-ee-die') is a powerful guarding breed from Morocco's Atlas mountains, a range of peaks that separate the country's coast from the vast Sahara desert. Aidis are sometimes described as sheepdogs, but they don't herd – the job of these alert pups is to protect a flock of sheep or goats from predators such as jackals. They are often used as watchdogs by nomadic tribes, too.

Aidis also make great tracking dogs and are sometimes partnered with the sloughi on hunts – the aidi sniffs out the prey and the sloughi chases after it. Although they can be kept as pets, aidis are wanderers at heart and need a good amount of space and exercise to keep them happy.

POOCH PROFILE:
Country: Morocco **Size:** Large; 52–62 cm (20–24 in) tall **Coat:** Medium-length, dense coat; various colours including white, black, black and white, brown **Personality:** Independent, protective, brave

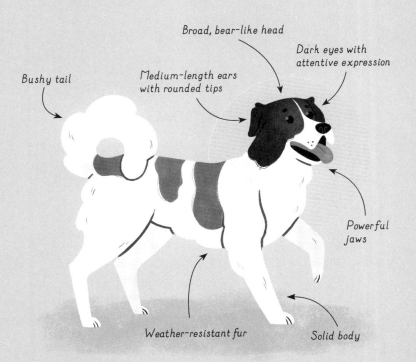

Broad, bear-like head

Dark eyes with attentive expression

Bushy tail

Medium-length ears with rounded tips

Powerful jaws

Weather-resistant fur

Solid body

The aidi has an unusually thick coat for an African breed. Its dense fur protects the dog from the changeable weather in its mountain home and shields it from the blisteringly hot Sun.

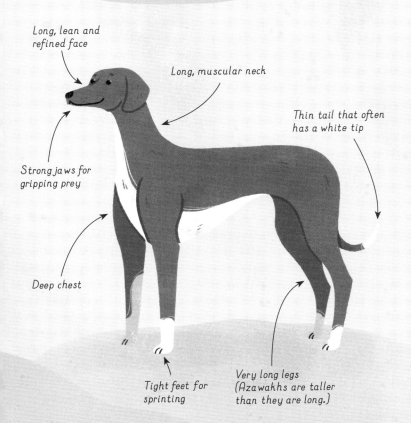

Long, lean and refined face

Long, muscular neck

Thin tail that often has a white tip

Strong jaws for gripping prey

Deep chest

Tight feet for sprinting

Very long legs (Azawakhs are taller than they are long.)

AZAWAKH

This tall, supple sighthound is a sprinter supreme and companion to the nomadic tribes of the Sahara. The breed was developed in the deserts of Burkina Faso, Mali and Niger, and an Azawakh ('as-a-wak') is most at home zooming across scorching-hot sands after an antelope. Rather than pursue prey on their own like other sighthounds, Azawakhs hunt in groups, chasing down their target until it's worn out.

Azawakhs are treasured as hunters and guardians in their home countries, and treated as important members of the family. Although tough and tireless on a hunt, these dogs are sensitive souls and form close bonds with their owners.

POOCH PROFILE:
Country: Burkina Faso, Mali and Niger **Size:** Large–Giant; 60–74 cm (23–29 in) tall **Coat:** Short and fine; light sand to dark mahogany and brindle **Personality:** Hardy, sensitive, loyal

WILD DOGS

Although they look very different, every dog in this book – from the sausage-shaped dachshund to the slobbery St Bernard – is descended from just one ancient species of wolf. Dogs and wolves belong to a group of animals known as canines, and their family tree includes other dog-like creatures, such as jackals, foxes and coyotes. Here are just a few of your furr-ever friend's wild cousins.

GREY WOLF
(North America, Europe and Asia)

The grey wolf is the closest wild relative to the pampered pooch on your sofa. Like a pet dog, a wolf has a keen sense of smell and sharp hearing, growls when its angry and wags its tail when it's happy. Wolves live in family groups, called packs, of around 6 to 10 individuals. A pack is normally led by an older male and female couple, but the whole family work as a team to raise pups and hunt. Each pack has its own special howl. When a pack howls together, they can be heard for up to 16 km (10 miles)!

GOLDEN JACKAL
(Europe and Asia)

These adaptable canines are found across southern Asia and in southeast Europe. They tend to hunt alone and will eat pretty much anything, from rodents, birds and reptiles to insects, fruit and plants. Golden jackals live in small family groups. Like wolves, groups of jackals will howl together to tell other jackals where they are and to mark their territory. Adults howl standing up, while puppies howl sitting down!

AFRICAN WILD DOG
(Southern and Eastern Africa)

Covered from head to paw in splodges of red, black, brown, white and yellow fur, these colourful canines are also known as painted wolves or African painted dogs. Each dog has a completely unique pattern, like fingerprints on a human. Large packs of African wild dogs once roamed across Africa, but their numbers have been hit by hunting and habitat loss. Today, this big-eared canine is one of the world's most endangered mammals.

DHOLE (Central, Southern and Eastern Asia)

Deep within the jungles and alpine forests of Asia lives a mysterious canine called the dhole (pronounced 'dole'). About as big as a medium-sized dog, with a long back and rust-red coat, dholes look very similar to foxes. They communicate using a high-pitched cry that sounds more like the call of a bird than that of a dog and has given them the nickname of 'the Asian whistling dog'. Threatened by habitat loss, there are thought to only be around 2,000 adult dholes in the wild.

DINGO (Australia)

Dingoes are wild dogs that have been roaming the Australian outback for at least 4,000 years. They are thought to be descended from domestic dogs that travelled with prehistoric settlers from Asia to Australia. Dingoes appear often in Aboriginal Australian myths as guardians of homes and protectors against evil spirits. They are Australia's top predators and usually hunt small animals, such as rabbits and lizards, but sometimes packs will take on bigger prey, like kangaroos.

MANED WOLF (South America)

The maned wolf looks like a fox on stilts, but it's neither a fox nor a wolf – it's a canine species all of its own. They are named after the furry ruff around their necks, which sticks up when the animal senses danger or is excited. They live on plains where their long legs give them just enough height to see across the tall grasses and their big ears allow them to listen out for rodents and rabbits. Small animals and birds form a big part of a maned wolf's diet, but it will also eat fruit, tubers and sugar cane.

Wrinkly forehead with a quizzical expression

Strong jaws

Curled tail

Stiff, upright ears

Slim waist

Brisk, busy stride when walking

Small, nimble feet

BASENJI

Can't choose between dogs and cats? Then the basenji ('ba-sen-jee') may be the pooch for you. These one-of-a-kind dogs are often compared to cats because they are quick on their feet, like to do their own thing and keep themselves spotlessly clean. Basenjis are also known for lacking an essential doggie trait – they don't bark. If you knock on a basenji's front door, you'll be greeted by a yodel instead!

Used to track birds and small animals in forests along the Congo river, the basenji is thought to be one of the oldest breeds in the world and appears on ancient Babylonian and Egyptian artworks. Thanks to their remote rainforest home, the look and character of the breed has stayed the same over the centuries. Basenjis perched on sofas today are pretty much identical to the dogs that befriended the pharaohs thousands of years ago.

POOCH PROFILE:

Country: Democratic Republic of the Congo
Size: Medium; 40–43 cm (16–17 in) tall **Coat:** Short and sleek; red and white, black and white, tricolour, or brindle and white **Personality:** Independent, curious, tidy

Brushing regularly is a must to keep coat smart and tangle free.

Long, fluffy coat with cotton-like texture

Feathery, curved tail

Dark eyes

Robust body

Black nose

Tight feet with black paw pads

COTON DE TULEAR

The cheerful Coton de Tulear ('co-tone dee too-lay-are') comes from the island of Madagascar, off Africa's east coast. As its name suggests, this dog has hair as soft and fluffy as a cotton ball. 'Tulear' refers to the island's port city of Tulear (now called Toliara) where the breed was developed.

No one is quite sure how these little white dogs first came to Madagascar but, like their cousin the Maltese (p65), they probably hitched a ride on the ships of merchants and sailors – though legend has it that a group of plucky Cotons were shipwrecked and swam ashore. After catching the eye of the island's royalty, they became cherished lapdogs, but were unknown outside of Madagascar until the 1960s, when French tourists started to bring the dogs home with them. Sweet and comical, Cotons make brilliant companions that will follow you from room to room and greet everyone they meet with licks rather than yaps!

POOCH PROFILE:

Country: Madagascar **Size:** Small; 22–30 cm (8–11 in) tall **Coat:** Long, supple and fluffy; usually all white, but can have grey or apricot shading on ears **Personality:** Friendly, outgoing, loyal

RHODESIAN RIDGEBACK

If you meet a Rhodesian ridgeback, the first thing you're likely to notice is the long strip of sticky-up fur running along its back. This fur gives the dog the second half of its name. The first half refers to Southern Rhodesia, a region in Africa that is now the country of Zimbabwe. This is where these hounds were first bred by Dutch settlers to track down large animals, including lions.

As you'd expect from a dog that's a match for the king of the beasts, ridgebacks are athletic and fearless. They are thought to be the result of crossing large European breeds, including greyhounds, mastiffs and Great Danes, with dogs that belonged to the local Khoikhoi people. The Khoikhoi's dogs had ridges down their backs, which were seen as signs of courage.

Ridge of hair that grows in the opposite direction to the rest of the dog's coat

Sparkling eyes

Tail carried with a slight curve

Large, strong teeth

Muscular, strong-boned legs

Compact feet with fur between pads for protection on rough ground

Ridgebacks can be stubborn and unaware of their size. But despite their powerful image, they are good-natured dogs that are faithful and snuggly with people they love. A bit like a lion in dog's clothing, ridgebacks combine strength with bags of loyalty to their family pack.

POOCH PROFILE:

Country: Zimbabwe **Size:** Large; 61–69 cm (24–27 in) tall **Coat:** Short and glossy; varieties of wheaten, from light to deep red **Personality:** Dignified, smart, affectionate

RECORD-BREAKING DOGS

As a canine superfan, you know dogs are great. But do you know just how incredible they are? Have a read of these mind-blowing feats and facts, and you'll never look at your furry best friend in quite the same way again.

CLEVER CANINE

Border collies often come out top in studies of dog intelligence. A collie called Chaser from South Carolina, USA, holds the world record for the most words understood by a dog – clever Chaser was able to recognise the names of (and go fetch) a whopping 1,022 toys.

GOLDEN OLDIE

The oldest known dog, according to Guinness World Records, was an Australian cattle dog called Bluey who lived in Victoria in Australia. This long-lived dog was born in 1910 and died in November 1939 at the age of 29 years and 5 months. The average dog lives for around 10–13 years, though smaller breeds can live up to around 18 years.

HIGH JUMP

In 2017, a greyhound called Feather from Maryland, USA, took the title of 'highest jump by a dog', when she leapt an incredible 191.7 cm (75.5 in). That's more than twice the height of an average greyhound.

Did You Know?
Like a human's fingerprint, a dog's nose print is unique.

Did You Know?
Dogs can catch yawns from humans. This is thought to be a sign that dogs can demonstrate empathy – the ability to understand and be sensitive to another being's feelings.

ECO HERO

A Labrador from Wales called Tubby helped his owner recycle a record-breaking 26,000 plastic bottles over the course of six years. Tubby picked up the bottles on his daily walks, and is believed to have recycled thousands more during his lifetime.

ROOM FOR ONE MORE?

The current record-holder for 'most tennis balls held in the mouth by a dog' is a golden retriever called Finley from New York State, USA. He held six regular-sized tennis balls in his mouth at once!

ALL THE BETTER TO LICK YOU WITH!

Brandy, a boxer from Michigan, USA, licked her way into the record books in 2002 with a super-long tongue that measured 43 cm (17 in).

WAG-TASTIC

An Irish wolfhound called Keon from Belgium holds the world record for the longest tail. Keon's tail measured a whopping 76.8 cm (30.2 in) long. Imagine being greeted by this super wagger!

Did You Know?
All dogs dream when they sleep. Studies suggest that smaller breeds dream frequently, but their dreams tend to be short. Larger breeds don't dream as often but they have longer dreams when they do.

DON'T MESS WITH MIDGE!

A Chihuahua cross called Midge holds the world record for 'smallest police dog'. Measuring just 28 cm (11 in) tall and 58 cm (23 in) long, little Midge spent 10 years using her super senses to help police in Ohio, USA, detect illegal drugs. She retired in 2016.

1. **SALUKI** IRAN, IRAQ AND SYRIA
2. **ANATOLIAN SHEPHERD DOG** TURKEY
3. **CANAAN DOG** ISRAEL AND THE PALESTINIAN TERRITORIES
4. **AFGHAN HOUND** AFGHANISTAN
5. **BORZOI** RUSSIA
6. **RUSSIAN BLACK TERRIER** RUSSIA
7. **SAMOYED** RUSSIA
8. **SIBERIAN HUSKY** RUSSIA
9. **CHOW CHOW** CHINA
10. **SHAR PEI** CHINA
11. **PEKINGESE** CHINA
12. **CHINESE CRESTED DOG** CHINA
13. **PUG** CHINA
14. **SHIH TZU** CHINA
15. **LHASA APSO** CHINA
16. **TIBETAN TERRIER** CHINA
17. **TIBETAN SPANIEL** CHINA
18. **RAMPUR GREYHOUND** INDIA
19. **TAIWAN DOG** TAIWAN
20. **JINDO** SOUTH KOREA
21. **THAI RIDGEBACK** THAILAND
22. **AKITA INU** JAPAN
23. **SHIBA INU** JAPAN
24. **JAPANESE CHIN** JAPAN
25. **JAPANESE SPITZ** JAPAN

6.

5.

17.

2.

1.

4.

14.

3.

ASIA

· · · · · · · · · · · · · · · ·

Many Asian dog breeds were developed inside tightly guarded palaces and remote mountain monasteries — one was even created thanks to a top-secret breeding programme. As a result, these pooches have a look and character that is all their own. Despite their isolated origins, today these canines number among the most popular breeds on the planet. From lovable lapdogs and loyal guardians to lightning-quick sighthounds and sturdy sledge pullers, Asia has a doggie for everyone.

Salukis were best buds of ancient Egyptian pharaohs and are sometimes known as the 'royal dog of Egypt'.

7.

8.

A husky's eyes can come in different colours – it's common for a husky to have one blue eye and one brown eye.

Scientists have discovered that shar peis have an unusual gene that causes their skin to be loose and baggy. Shar pei puppies are much more wrinkly than adults. The dog's skin gets smoother as it matures.

13.

22.

10.

11.

24.

16.

9.

20.

23.

15.

25.

12.

19.

18.

A group of Jindos appeared in the opening ceremony of the 1988 Olympics in Seoul, South Korea.

21.

When a new baby is born, Japanese parents are traditionally presented with a small statue of an Akita, which symbolises health, happiness and long life for their child.

The nomadic tribes that created the saluki believed the dog was a gift from God and called the breed 'the noble one'.

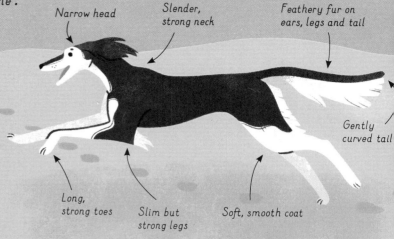

Narrow head

Slender, strong neck

Feathery fur on ears, legs and tail

Gently curved tail

Long, strong toes

Slim but strong legs

Soft, smooth coat

SALUKI

An ancient breed, the saluki has been prized by pharaohs, kings and tribal chieftains in Africa and the Middle East for the last 5,000 years. They were originally bred as hunting dogs. Packs of saluki would have been taken out into the desert alongside riders on horseback to chase down gazelle, fox and hare. A saluki's far-seeing eyes are made for gazing across desert dunes.

Graceful and athletic, the saluki is the dancer of the doggie world. A notable feature is their elegant, thin feet and long middle toes, which help the dogs to maintain speed and steer across shifting sands. These quiet dogs can seem stand-offish with strangers, but they form very deep attachments with those they love.

POOCH PROFILE:

Country: Iran, Iraq and Syria **Size:** Large; 58–71 cm (23–28 in) tall **Coat:** Smooth or smooth with feathery legs, ears and tail; various colours including cream, fawn, red, black, and black and tan **Personality:** Elegant, sensitive, independent

Floppy, triangular ears

Large, heavy head

Dark ears and dark mask on face

Strong teeth

Long tail, carried low when resting and curled high over back when alert

Thick fur with dense undercoat

Powerful, muscular body and legs

POOCH PROFILE:

Country: Turkey **Size:** Large–Giant; 71–81 cm (28–32 in) tall **Coat:** Short and thick; comes in various colours but the most traditional is fawn with black face markings **Personality:** Steady, intelligent, bold

ANATOLIAN SHEPHERD DOG

The Anatolian shepherd dog takes its name from an ancient region of Turkey called Anatolia, where it has been used as a guardian of sheep and goats since around 2000 BCE. These thick-built yet agile dogs are especially suited to the rugged highlands and mountain peaks of Central Anatolia. Their dense double coat means they can happily plod behind the flock in all weathers.

These calm canines prefer to use their sheer size to see off threats to their flock rather than start a fight. This has made the breed a popular choice for conservation programmes working to save endangered predators. Farmers in the southern African country of Namibia, for instance, use Anatolian shepherds to guard their sheep from cheetahs, instead of traps or guns. Any cheetah approaching the flock is put off by the presence of the dog and goes elsewhere to hunt, allowing the farmers and the big cats to live side by side.

CANAAN DOG

With fur the colour of desert sands, the Canaan dog is the national breed of Israel. The ancestors of the Canaan are thought to have been the dogs used by ancient Jewish communities to herd sheep and guard homes. When the Romans destroyed the city of Jerusalem in 70 CE, the Jewish people were forced to flee their homeland and their dogs were left to fend for themselves in the desert.

These hardy dogs lived a semi-wild life until the early 1900s, when a breeding programme was set up to tame them. The Canaan has since become much loved in its home country. Adaptable and clever, they can turn their sharp brains to all sorts of tasks. Over the last century, these have included carrying messages to troops, detecting unexploded mines for the military and working as police dogs.

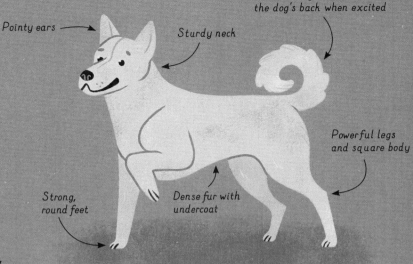

Pointy ears

Sturdy neck

Thick, bushy tail, curled over the dog's back when excited

Powerful legs and square body

Strong, round feet

Dense fur with undercoat

POOCH PROFILE:

Country: Israel and the Palestinian Territories
Size: Large; 50–60 cm (20–24 in) tall **Coat:** Short- to medium-length; usually sandy in colour but can also be red, white, black or spotted **Personality:** Confident, independent, watchful

Long face

Silky, fine hair

Tip of the tail curls into a ring

Head held proudly on long neck

Needs brushing every day!

Long, strong legs

Large paw pads act as shock absorbers

AFGHAN HOUND

Swishing its stunning coat, in floats one of the canine world's superstars – the Afghan hound. Although the origins of this beautiful breed are uncertain, these silky sighthounds have been dashing across the deserts of Afghanistan for thousands of years. They're thought to be closely related to salukis (see opposite), whose feathery fur may have provided the basis for the Afghan's show-stopping hair.

Beneath those luxurious locks is a fast, fierce hunter. Originally used to chase gazelle and leopards across the plains and mountains of Afghanistan, their wildness has never been totally tamed. When it wishes, an Afghan hound can be sweetly silly and affectionate towards those it loves. But most of the time, it will gaze through you with a dreamy indifference. You don't own an Afghan hound – it owns you!

POOCH PROFILE:

Country: Afghanistan **Size:** Large; 63–74 cm (25–29 in) tall **Coat:** Very long, fine hair; various colours including cream, black and tan, red and white **Personality:** Elegant, aloof, mischievous

Very slim, narrow head

Arched neck

Long, powerful jaws for catching wolves

Long, feathery tail

Muscular legs for speed

Silky fur with a thick undercoat to keep the dog warm in Russian winters

BORZOI

Once prized by Russian royalty, the borzoi was developed in the 1600s by crossing sighthounds similar to greyhounds (p41) with long-haired sheepdogs. Beneath the beauty of a borzoi's wavy coat is a formidable beast, bred by Russian aristocrats to chase and catch wolves. A wolf hunt was a grand affair, often lasting for days and ending with a lavish feast. When Russia's aristocracy was overturned following the Russian Revolution of 1917, borzois almost went extinct, but the breed was saved by fans abroad.

A borzoi is a sensitive soul that likes to stick by the side of its favourite person. However, they can be aloof, and will peer disapprovingly down their long nose if they don't want to do something. This princely pooch is happiest in a household with a long couch to stretch its elegant body and lots of outdoor space to show off its speed – its name comes from a Russian word for 'fast'.

POOCH PROFILE:
Country: Russia **Size:** Large; at least 68 cm (27 in) tall
Coat: Silky, wavy or curly; various colours, including black and cream, gold, brindle and white **Personality:** Sensitive, dignified, fast

RUSSIAN BLACK TERRIER

In the late 1940s, in a top-secret location outside of Moscow, Russia's Communist government set up a breeding programme to create a strong, hard-working dog. During the chaos and destruction of the Russian Revolution and two world wars, many Russian breeds had died out and the country found itself without any dogs that were suitable for a tough life in the military and police.

Around 17 different breeds, including giant schnauzers (p52), Airedales (p55), Rottweilers (p53) and Newfoundlands (p13), went into the mix that made the Russian black terrier. This new breed was big, brawny and beardy, with a thick coat to keep out the cold while on patrol during bleak winter nights. Originally used as police and guard dogs, Russian black terriers have been kept as pets since the 1950s. This protective pooch won't want to share you with strangers, but it will always have your back.

Triangular ears

Big, broad skull

Large black nose

Thick tail that sometimes curls over the back

Muscular neck legs and body

Weatherproof fur with thick undercoat

POOCH PROFILE:
Country: Russia **Size:** Large–Giant; 66–77 cm (26–30 in) tall **Coat:** Medium-length, slightly wavy; black
Personality: Protective, confident, even-tempered

Strong neck and shoulders for pulling sledges

Wedge-shaped head

Black lips and nose

Furry tail, often carried over the back

Muscular legs

Deep chest

Very thick, soft fur – needs daily brushing

SAMOYED

The smiley Samoyed is a dog that brings happiness and a lot of hair wherever it goes. Despite looking like a walking fluffball, these dogs were originally bred to pull sledges and herd reindeer for the Samoyedic people, a nomadic tribe in north-eastern Siberia. Happiest when in a pack, Samoyeds are social characters that like to say hello to everyone (human or dog) they pass in the street.

Everything about these cuddly pooches is tailored to withstand some of the most brutal weather conditions on the planet – winter temperatures in Siberia can drop to a teeth-chattering –22°C (–7°F). To protect them, Samoyeds have a dense double coat that covers every inch of their body. Even their ears and the gaps between their toes are lined with fur. A Samoyed's signature 'smile' also has a practical purpose, as the upturned corners of the dog's mouth stop slobber from escaping and freezing into icicles.

POOCH PROFILE:
Country: Russia **Size:** Medium–Large; 46–56 cm (18–22 in) tall **Coat:** Dense fur; pure white **Personality:** Affectionate, active, intelligent

SIBERIAN HUSKY

One of the most popular sled dogs in the world, the Siberian husky is a beautiful wolf-like breed from north-east Russia. They were originally bred by the Chukchi people of Siberia to pull sledges over long distances in their remote snowy home. In the early 1900s, huskies were imported to Alaska where they were raced against Malamutes (p16) and made their name as the fastest dogs on the ice.

Built for pounding across frozen plains, huskies are not a dog for sitting still. They are energetic, intelligent animals that love to join their humans on jogs or, better still, take part in dryland sledging (if snow is in short supply). Second to pulling a sledge, a husky's favourite place to be is with its pack. If you succeed in wearing your husky out, they'll gladly have a snooze with you on the sofa … just make it a short one because this dog has places to go!

Wolfish appearance

Straight and strong body

Bushy, brush-like tail

Walks quickly and lightly

Muscly legs

Smooth topcoat and soft undercoat

Compact feet with fur between toes

POOCH PROFILE:
Country: Russia **Size:** Large; 51–60 cm (20–23 in) tall **Coat:** Medium-length, dense coat; various colours, including white, black and white, brown and white, and grey and white **Personality:** Good-natured, energetic, sociable

A PUP'S LIFE

Cuddly, cheeky, downright adorable ... it's impossible not to love puppies. But they don't stay teeny for long! A lot goes on in the first year of a pup's life and there are important milestones each puppy should experience so it can grow into a well-rounded and happy adult dog. Let's follow one pup for a year and see what he gets up to.

Mother dogs give birth to several puppies at once, called a 'litter'. The size of a litter depends on the breed of dog – bigger dogs tend to have bigger litters – but the average number of pups in a litter is around 6. The largest litter of puppies ever recorded was 24! This mega bundle of cuteness was born to a Neapolitan mastiff called Tia in November 2004.

Newborn: 0-4 weeks

Meet Mojo. This little pup has just been born. He is very small and completely dependent on his mum for milk, care and warmth. Mojo's eyes and ears are closed, but he can crawl and makes lots of squeaky noises to get his mum's attention. By about week 2, his eyes and ears will have started to open and he will begin to interact with his brothers and sisters.

First walks and wags: 4-8 weeks

At the age of 4 weeks, Mojo looks more puppy-like – and is getting into plenty of mischief! He's walking, wagging his tail and even giving barking a go. He'll have sharp baby teeth by now and will have had his first taste of solid food. During this stage, Mojo will be picking up doggie manners from his mum, and will be practising social skills by playing with his siblings.

Making friends: 8-12 weeks

By now, Mojo is big enough to leave his mum and go to his new human family. Exciting! He's had his first vaccinations – one at 8 weeks and another at 12 weeks. These protect Mojo from dog diseases, making it safe for him to meet other dogs and be taken to public places. It's important for Mojo to meet new people and friendly older dogs at this age, so he can learn good doggie behaviours. His humans also gently introduce him to different places – such as parks, shops and railway stations – so he can get used to the big wide world.

Pup school:
12 weeks-6 months

Mojo's humans will start taking him to training classes when he's about 16 weeks old. This is a great way for Mojo to meet other puppies and develop his social skills, as well as start to learn commands. During this period, Mojo is toilet trained, too (so much to learn!). Mojo's adult teeth will also start to grow around now, replacing his baby teeth. Getting grown-up dog teeth is a painful business, so Mojo will chew anything he can get his paws on to soothe his achy mouth. Slippers, beware …

Teen time: 6-12 months

Uh oh … Mojo's hit his teens and he wants to test boundaries. Teenage dogs are more independent and confident than puppies and they have a lot of energy to burn – if it's not channelled properly, this can get them into trouble. Mojo's humans keep him busy with lots of playtime and exercise and keep up his positive training.

All grown up: 1 year old

Happy birthday, Mojo! At one year old, Mojo has matured into an adult dog. He's still got a cheeky puppy side, but thanks to a lot of training and love from his humans, he's settled down into a trusty member of the family.

CHOW CHOW

According to Chinese legend, the unusual blue-black colour of a chow chow's tongue can be traced back to the dawn of time, when a curious dog licked the sky as it was being painted. They are certainly an ancient breed. Dogs similar to chows feature in the pottery and sculptures of China's Han Dynasty (206 BCE–220 CE), where they are shown as sturdy hunters and guardians.

Chows have lots of stamina, but they take their time over things. They have a distinctive stiff-legged walk and a serious manner about them – this is not a dog that's going to do silly zoomies in the park. And while their fabulous manes and coats make them look perfect for cuddling, chows like their space. This noble dog is happiest standing dependably at your side, just as its ancestors would have stood by Chinese emperors thousands of years ago.

Small, thick ears that tilt over the eyes, creating a stern expression

Broad head

Strong neck that carries the head proudly

Tail curls well over back

Black mouth, gums and tongue

Sturdy legs

Very dense fur

POOCH PROFILE:
Country: China **Size:** Medium–Large; 46–56 cm (18–22 in) tall **Coat:** Thick coat; black, red, blue, fawn or cream **Personality:** Dignified, loyal, strong-willed

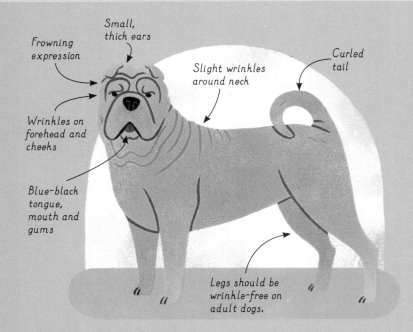

Frowning expression

Small, thick ears

Slight wrinkles around neck

Curled tail

Wrinkles on forehead and cheeks

Blue-black tongue, mouth and gums

Legs should be wrinkle-free on adult dogs.

POOCH PROFILE:
Country: China **Size:** Medium; 46–51 cm (18–20 in) tall **Coat:** Harsh, bristly coat with loose skin; various colours including black, grey, brown, cream and red **Personality:** Dignified, independent, calm

SHAR PEI

This prune-like pooch may look like it's spent too long in a bathtub, but it has a majestic history that stretches back to ancient China. Like chow chows, shar peis are thought to be descended from dogs that guarded homes and temples during the Han Dynasty. The shar pei shares the chow chow's blue-black tongue and scowly expression, but instead of a teddy-bear coat, it has short fur and folded skin. If you stroke a shar pei, you'll notice its coat feels surprisingly bristly, and it's this that gives the breed its name – 'shar pei' comes from a Mandarin word meaning 'sandpaper skin'.

The shar peis that were originally used as guard dogs and, later, fighting dogs, had smoother skin and longer jaws than those of today. A modern shar pei's wrinkles and soft mouth are the result of breeding programmes in the 1970s, when shar peis were crossed with flatter-faced breeds, such as bulldogs (p41) and pugs (p90). Steadfast and serene, the shar pei makes a trusty guardian of your sofa.

PEKINGESE

Chinese legends tell how the Pekingese (or 'Peke') was created by the Buddha, who shrunk a lion to the size of a marmoset monkey. With a proud face framed by a magnificent furry mane, this dog looks every inch the little lion.

The origins of these fluffy lapdogs are uncertain but they are named after Peking (now Beijing), the Chinese capital, and their thick fur is perfectly suited to the city's chilly winter climate. Not that Pekingeses would have spent much time shivering outside. Treasured by emperors since the 8th century CE, Pekes were bred as companions and watchdogs for the rich and powerful and could only be owned by those who lived within the walls of the Chinese Imperial Palace.

Today, Pekes will trot round an apartment with a dignified, rolling walk, and still expect to be treated like royalty. These dogs demand a lot of care – not least a daily brush – but they reward their human subjects with lion-like devotion.

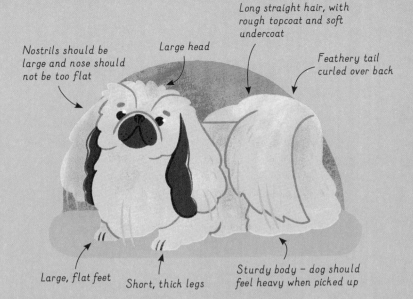

Nostrils should be large and nose should not be too flat

Large head

Long straight hair, with rough topcoat and soft undercoat

Feathery tail curled over back

Large, flat feet

Short, thick legs

Sturdy body – dog should feel heavy when picked up

POOCH PROFILE:
Country: China **Size:** Small; 15–22 cm (6–9 in) tall
Coat: Long, dense hair; colours include black and tan, cream and brindle **Personality:** Noble, affectionate, strong-willed

Large, sticky-up ears

Graceful neck

Well-shaped face

Smooth skin that is warm to the touch

Slender body

Long feet

POOCH PROFILE:
Country: China **Size:** Small; 23–33 cm (9–13 in) tall
Coat: Hairless body with fur on head, feet and tail, or fully coated **Personality:** Cheerful, alert, lively

CHINESE CRESTED DOG

Sporting furry flares, a mop of hair and a whole lot of attitude, there's something a bit rock 'n' roll about the Chinese crested dog. Its ancestors are thought to have been much larger and probably came from Africa rather than China. But it was in the palaces of Chinese emperors that the breed was miniaturised, and on the ships of Chinese sailors that these dogs spread across the world. Crested dogs won't say no to a warm lap, but remember that they made their name as rat-catchers – so they will enjoy a run round an agility course.

There are two types of crested dogs – one is largely hairless, the other is covered from nose to tail in fluff. The amount of hair on hairless crested dogs can vary, but they usually only have hair on their heads, on the tips of their tails and around their feet. Their floofier siblings are covered in a fine coat of soft, silky hair, and are known as 'powder puffs'. Litters can contain both hairy and non-hairy puppies.

PUG

The cheery pug is the lord of the lapdogs. But for a pooch that likes to sit still, it has an impressive number of miles under its paws. Originally bred more than 2,000 years ago as a cuddly companion for Chinese royalty and Buddhist monks, pugs were brought to Europe during the 1600s by Dutch merchants. They quickly snuggled their way on to the laps of kings, queens and aristocrats across the continent. Today, they are popular with city dwellers around the world due to their small size and bubbly personalities.

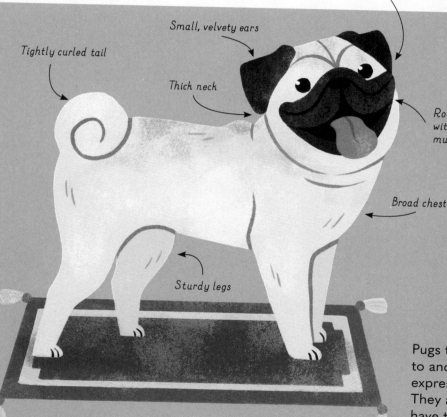

Large eyes with a soft expression

Small, velvety ears

Tightly curled tail

Thick neck

Round head with short muzzle

Broad chest

Sturdy legs

The origin of the word 'pug' is unknown, but the dogs may have got their name because they look a bit like marmoset monkeys, which were known as 'pug monkeys' and were popular pets in the 1700s. Another theory is that the name comes from a Latin word, *pugnus*, meaning 'fist', as the dog's squishy face was thought to resemble a clenched hand.

Pugs think they should be involved in whatever you're up to and this sweet self-importance, combined with their expressive, wrinkly faces, gives them a comical manner. They are snoozy dogs if left to their own devices and always have their eye on the treat tin, so they should have regular walks to keep them trim. Because their flat noses can cause breathing problems, any exercise should be gentle.

Ancient Chinese breeders gave meanings to the wrinkles on a pug's forehead. Dogs that had a pattern of wrinkles similar to the Chinese symbol for 'prince' – one vertical crease crossed by three horizontal lines – were thought to be particularly special.

POOCH PROFILE:
Country: China **Size:** Small; 25–33 cm (10–13 in) tall
Coat: Short and glossy coat; fawn, apricot, silver or black **Personality:** Friendly, adaptable, jolly

Very feathery tail, carried proudly like a banner over the back

Large, drooping ears

Often has a white stripe, or 'blaze', of hair on forehead

Long beard and whiskers

Walks with smooth, bold strides

Firm, round feet

Sturdy body and legs

Shih tzus are possibly the result of crossing Lhasa apsos (see below) with Pekingeses (p89).

SHIH TZU

Shih tzus ('sheet-sues') were made for a life of trotting round palaces after emperors. With their button noses held high in the air, these dogs can seem slightly stuck-up at first glance, but don't let that put you off – shih tzus are fun-loving pooches that want to be everyone's friend. Their bubbly personalities and love of a cuddle make them especially good therapy dogs (p60).

The name 'shih tzu' means 'lion dog', which is thought to be a reference to a Chinese folktale about a little dog that accompanied the Buddha on his travels and could transform into a lion to protect him. They're also known as 'chrysanthemum-faced dogs', because the hair on their heads grows upwards from the nose in a way that looks like the delicate petals of a chrysanthemum flower. If a shih tzu's hair is left to grow long, owners usually tie it up in a bun, which adds to the dog's stately style.

POOCH PROFILE:
Country: China **Size:** Small; 27 cm (10 in) tall
Coat: Long and dense; colours include black and white, silver and white, gold and brindle
Personality: Friendly, playful, outgoing

LHASA APSO

For centuries, Lhasa apsos have kept watch over Buddhist monasteries and temples in the remote Himalayan mountains of Tibet. They were used as indoor guardians, sounding the alarm if they heard a stranger approaching the front door and letting the larger mastiffs on the outside see the intruder off. As well as watchdogs, Lhasas were also sacred companions to the monks, who believed they might be reborn as monastery dogs when they died. Take a look into a Lhasa's soulful eyes and it's easy to understand why.

Lhasa apsos have surprisingly hard coats – they had to be tough to protect the dogs from the cold, windy climate of Tibet. Although a Lhasa with full floor-length locks is a glamorous sight, the dog underneath is a hardy one that will happily trot beside you whatever the weather.

Floppy, feathery ears

High, feathery tail, carried over the dog's back

Long whiskers and beard

Round, firm feet

Heavy topcoat and undercoat

Long body (dog is longer than it is tall)

POOCH PROFILE:
Country: China **Size:** Small; 25 cm (10 in) tall
Coat: Long, straight coat; all kinds of colours, including gold, sand, grey, black, white or brown
Personality: Alert, confident, cheerful

TIBETAN TERRIER

Tibetan terriers are not actually terriers at all. They started out as watchdogs in Buddhist monasteries – much like Lhasa apsos (p91), which they are related to. These nimble dogs also worked alongside shepherds, herding sheep across the mountains of Tibet. Their dense double coat kept them warm, and their large, flat, furry feet acted as natural snowshoes, helping the dogs climb the frosty peaks.

POOCH PROFILE:
Country: China **Size:** Small–Medium; 36–41 cm (14–16 in) tall **Coat:** Long, fine and dense coat; various colours, including white, gold, grey or a mix of shades **Personality:** Good-natured, active, alert

POOCH PROFILE:
Country: China **Size:** Small; 25 cm (10 in) tall
Coat: Silky topcoat and dense undercoat; all kinds of colours, including black and tan, red, gold and white
Personality: Happy-go-lucky, independent, loyal

TIBETAN SPANIEL

You guessed it – these little dogs aren't spaniels either! They originally lived (and still live) in Buddhist monasteries alongside Lhasa apsos and Tibetan terriers, where they helped keep watch and provided companionship for the monks. Their Tibetan name is simkhyi, which means 'house dog' or 'bedroom dog', and reflects their adored status. Like all of the breeds developed in Tibetan monasteries, these precious dogs were never sold – and receiving one as a gift was considered a great honour.

RAMPUR GREYHOUND

The Rampur ('rahm-poor') greyhound is named after a region of northern India, where it was developed during the 18th and 19th centuries. The breed is thought to have been created by local maharajahs (rulers), who crossed Afghan hounds with English greyhounds to make a solidly built yet speedy sighthound. These powerful dogs were mainly used to hunt large prey, such as deer, wild boar and jackals. Today, Rampur greyhounds are a very rare breed even in their home country.

POOCH PROFILE:
Country: India **Size:** Large; 56–76 cm (22–30 in) tall
Coat: Short and smooth; colours include grey, tan and black **Personality:** Good tempered, protective

TAIWAN DOG

The Taiwan dog may be one of the oldest and rarest breeds on the planet. These ancient canines can be traced back to prehistoric hunting dogs that lived alongside Taiwan's indigenous peoples in the island's thickly forested mountains. Today, they are used as watchdogs and companions, though crossing with non-local breeds in recent centuries has made a purebred Taiwan dog hard to find. If you're lucky enough to meet one, you'll be able to tell because true Taiwan dogs usually have black markings on their tongue.

POOCH PROFILE:
Country: Taiwan **Size:** Medium–Large; 43–52 cm (17–20 in) tall **Coat:** Short, smooth coat; colours include black, brindle, fawn and white
Personality: Intelligent, loyal, alert

JINDO

The Jindo is named after a South Korean island where it developed in isolation for centuries. Jindos were originally used as hunting dogs by the islanders, but they have gained a reputation as extremely faithful and loving pets since reaching the mainland. This is illustrated by the story of Baekgu, a white Jindo that travelled more than 300 km (180 miles) to get back to her elderly owner in 1993. The Jindo is so precious in its home country that it has held special status as a 'Natural Treasure' since 1962.

POOCH PROFILE:
Country: South Korea **Size:** Medium–Large; 45–55 cm (18–22 in) tall **Coat:** Medium-length, double coat; fawn, brindle, white, black and tan, grey or black **Personality:** Faithful, watchful, bright

THAI RIDGEBACK

Like Rhodesian ridgebacks (p77), Thai ridgebacks get their name from a line of hair along their backs that grows in the opposite direction to the rest of their coat. These dogs were first recorded 350 years ago, but the breed is thought to be much older than that. Originally used to hunt and to guard carts and homes in remote communities in eastern Thailand, Thai ridgebacks weren't known beyond their home country until the 1970s. They are still very rare outside of Thailand. Bred to look after themselves when off duty, Thai ridgebacks are independent and intelligent dogs.

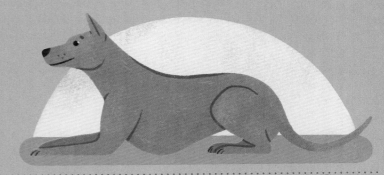

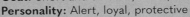

POOCH PROFILE:
Country: Thailand **Size:** Large; 51–61 cm (20–24 in) tall
Coat: Short and smooth; black, red, blue and brown
Personality: Alert, loyal, protective

SUPER DOGS

Although dogs come in many shapes and sizes, they all share a love of being around their human companions. Here are a few stories of heroic hounds who have gone the extra mile.

TOGO

In 1925, an outbreak of a deadly disease called diphtheria occurred in a small town in Alaska, USA. The infection was treated with a special medicine, but the nearest supply was 1,084 km (674 miles) away.

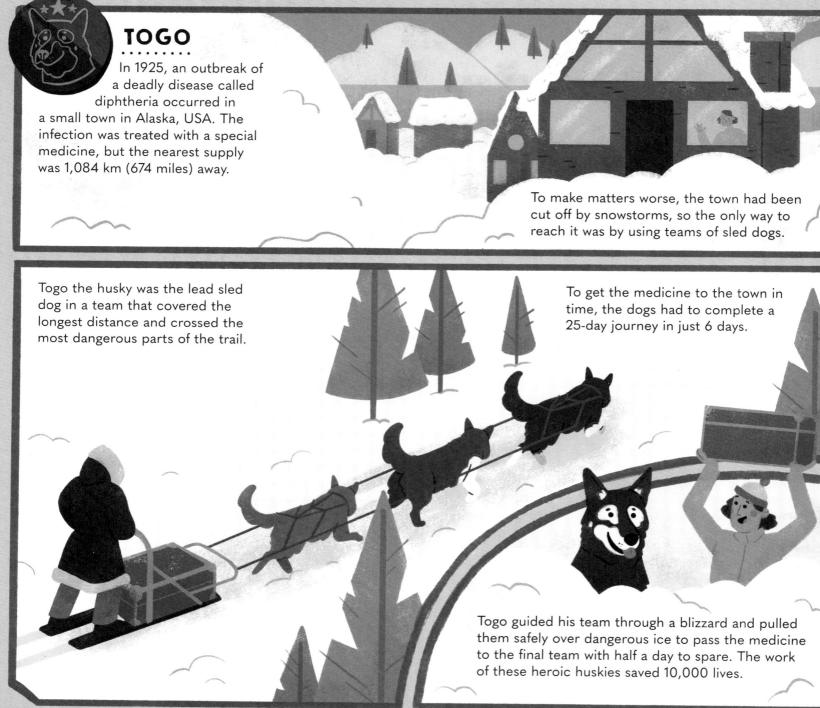

To make matters worse, the town had been cut off by snowstorms, so the only way to reach it was by using teams of sled dogs.

Togo the husky was the lead sled dog in a team that covered the longest distance and crossed the most dangerous parts of the trail.

To get the medicine to the town in time, the dogs had to complete a 25-day journey in just 6 days.

Togo guided his team through a blizzard and pulled them safely over dangerous ice to pass the medicine to the final team with half a day to spare. The work of these heroic huskies saved 10,000 lives.

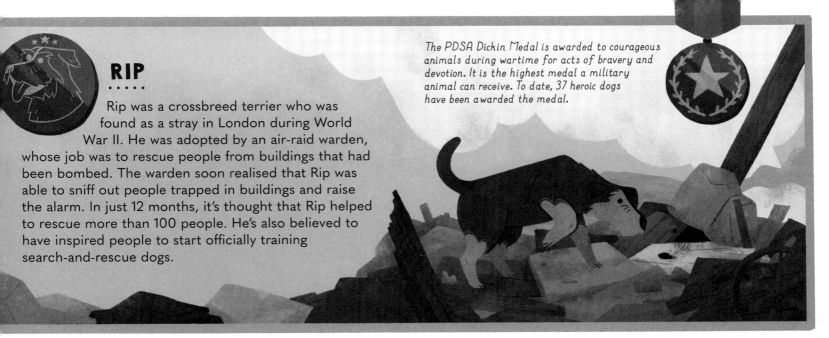

RIP

Rip was a crossbreed terrier who was found as a stray in London during World War II. He was adopted by an air-raid warden, whose job was to rescue people from buildings that had been bombed. The warden soon realised that Rip was able to sniff out people trapped in buildings and raise the alarm. In just 12 months, it's thought that Rip helped to rescue more than 100 people. He's also believed to have inspired people to start officially training search-and-rescue dogs.

The PDSA Dickin Medal is awarded to courageous animals during wartime for acts of bravery and devotion. It is the highest medal a military animal can receive. To date, 37 heroic dogs have been awarded the medal.

BEAR

Between 2019 and 2020, Australia was hit by the worst bushfires in the country's history. Millions of hectares of land were burnt, and the fires had a devastating effect on Australia's wildlife. In stepped Bear, a collie-koolie crossbreed who had a very special skill – using his nose to sniff out koalas trapped in the forests. Bear had been abandoned as a puppy but was rescued by a conservation team who trained him to use his sense of smell to find sick and injured koalas. Wearing socks to protect his paws on the burnt ground, Bear helped find more than 100 koalas in need. What a hero!

BABU

Twelve-year-old shih tzu Babu lived with her elderly owner in a town by the sea in Japan. Babu didn't usually like going for walks, but on a morning in March 2011, she insisted her owner take her out. As soon as they left the house, the little dog pulled her owner up a nearby hill – in the opposite direction to their normal walk. Minutes later, a giant wave known as a tsunami flooded the town and destroyed their home. Brave Babu had saved her owner's life.

AKITA INU

The Akita inu is one of six breeds that are celebrated as 'natural monuments' in Japan. The first part of its name comes from the mountainous Akita area of northern Japan (the 'inu' part means 'dog' in Japanese). More than three centuries ago, these hardy pooches were first developed there to hunt large prey, such as boar, deer and bear. They were also used to guard homes and later, as fighting dogs.

But a dog needs more than just muscle to achieve 'monument' status. The story of an Akita called Hachiko shows why the breed holds such a special place in the hearts of Japanese dog-lovers. Each day, for more than nine years, Hachiko walked to and from a train station in the hope that his beloved owner, who had died suddenly one day while at work, would return home. Akitas may be powerful, proud and sometimes stubborn, but they will go to the Moon and back for their favourite person – if that's you, you're a lucky human indeed.

Thick tail that curls tightly over the back

Strong, level back

Thick ears that tip slightly forwards

Broad skull

Muscly, well-boned legs

POOCH PROFILE:
Country: Japan **Size:** Large; 58–70 cm (22–27 in) tall
Coat: Dense, double coat; red, fawn, sesame (red and black), brindle and white **Personality:** Faithful, composed, courageous

Foxy face

Triangular ears that tip slightly forward

Thick tail that curls over back

Hard topcoat with soft undercoat

Muscly neck

Firm feet

POOCH PROFILE:
Country: Japan **Size:** Small–Medium; 35–41 cm (14–16 in) tall **Coat:** Dense and plush; white, red, black and tan, brindle and sesame **Personality:** Alert, bold, good-natured

SHIBA INU

The shiba inu ('she-ba ee-nu') is an ancient breed, believed to have been around since 300 BCE. Shibas originally came from the mountains of central Japan, where they were bred to chase birds and rabbits out of bushes and towards human hunters. The 'shiba' part of their name may refer to the dog's compact size – an old meaning of the word is 'small' – or to the brushwood thickets that these nimble pooches once zipped through on hunts.

Shibas are fox-like in appearance and cat-like in personality. They are free-thinking canines that like to do their own thing, take great pride in their plush coats and don't care much for getting their paws wet. Though not generally noisy, a shiba will often express excitement with a high-pitched, meow sound, also known as a 'shiba scream'. Their unique combination of sweetness and sass – that can only be described as 'shiba-ttude' – has made them one of the most popular breeds in Japan today.

JAPANESE CHIN

Japan is a country that treasures all of its 'inu', but it reserves an extra-special cushion for the chin. These pretty lapdogs are thought to have originated in ancient China or Korea and were probably given as gifts to Japan's royal family around 500–1,000 years ago. For the next few centuries, chins spent their days inside Japan's palaces, lounging on silk beds or peeping out from the sleeves of ladies' kimonos.

Though they are made for a life of luxury, chins won't turn their noses up at a scamper round the park and they have a silly side to them, too. If you say a magic word like 'dinner' or 'walk' to a chin, chances are they'll twirl around in circles with excitement. This sweet, signature move is nicknamed the 'chin spin'.

Chins like to groom themselves with their front paws like cats do, and have a habit of jumping on to high perches.

Tail curls over back

Feathery ears

Round head with a very short muzzle

Long, soft fur

Straight, slender legs

POOCH PROFILE:
Country: Japan **Size:** Small; 20–28 cm (8–11 in) tall
Coat: Straight and silky; either black and white or red and white **Personality:** Happy, gentle, lively

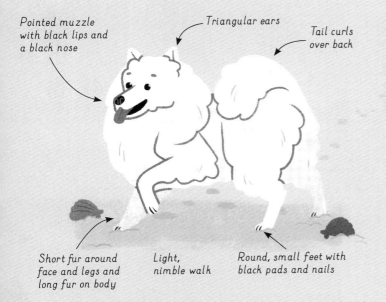

Pointed muzzle with black lips and a black nose

Triangular ears

Tail curls over back

Short fur around face and legs and long fur on body

Light, nimble walk

Round, small feet with black pads and nails

POOCH PROFILE:
Country: Japan **Size:** Small; 30–37 cm (12–14 in) tall **Coat:** Long, dense double coat; pure white **Personality:** Alert, friendly, intelligent

JAPANESE SPITZ

Compared to Japan's other breeds, the Japanese spitz is a relative newcomer. It was first developed in the 1920s and is thought to be the result of crossing various spitz breeds, including the German spitz and, possibly, the Samoyed (p85). With a coat that sparkles like freshly fallen snow and a happy-go-lucky attitude, it's hard not to fall under the spell of these friendly fluffballs.

Japanese spitzes are first and foremost companion dogs and their favourite place to be is with their family. They're active characters that will happily tag along with you on a walk or a run on the beach. Although their brilliant coat needs regular brushing to look its best, it's not difficult to groom or keep clean as it naturally repels dirt.

DOGS ON THE GO

Doggie sports are a fantastic way to burn off energy, keep a busy canine brain occupied and strengthen the bond between a dog and their human. Although some breeds are more suited to these activities than others, any dog can take part and, with time and positive training, master some truly amazing skills. On your barks, get set … go, go, go!

FLYBALL

Flyball is a fast, fun and noisy doggie sport. Teams of pooches race down a track, leaping over a series of jumps on the way, to reach a box of tennis balls. When a dog gets to the box, they have to press a trigger with their paws to release a ball, catch it and then run back to their team at top speed. The speediest team wins. Flyball is suited to energetic dogs, such as border collies and lurchers, but all shapes and sizes can get involved. Some dogs find flyball so exciting that they bark while they wait to have their go!

DANCING

If you've ever watched a dog show on TV, you might have seen dogs performing incredible dance routines with their humans. In the canine world, this sport is known as 'heelwork to music' or 'freestyle', and it combines obedience training with dance. In heelwork to music, dogs trot closely beside their human and mirror their moves. Anything goes in freestyle, with dogs performing fabulous tricks, including jumps, rolls, spins and leg weaving, in time to the music. If your dog is a superstar in the making, this might be the sport for them.

SCENTWORK

This sport channels a dog's natural smelling ability. It's based on the work of police sniffer dogs, which use their noses to find explosives or drugs. A dog is given a set amount of time to sniff out pieces of material that have been soaked in a natural oil and hidden around a search area. Once the dog has found the specific smell, it alerts its human handler. Because this activity requires a lot of focus, it can help to calm anxious dogs and increase the confidence of shyer dogs.

Simple scent games are a great way to exercise your dog's mind and to keep them active indoors on rainy days. Try hiding your dog's favourite toy or a particularly tasty treat in another room and then ask them to 'find it'!

AGILITY

In agility, a human handler guides their dog through an obstacle course made up of exciting challenges, including tunnels, jumps, see-saws and ramps. Dogs race against each other to finish the course in the quickest time. Any breed can try their paw at agility for fun and to keep fit. Teaching your dog to do simple agility activities at home – such as leaping through a hula hoop – is also a great way to have a work-out with your canine chum.

If you fancy a dog activity that's a little more relaxing, consider yoga (or 'doga'). An Australian shepherd dog called Secret took the internet by storm in 2021 when she was filmed doing a yoga routine with her owner. As well as yoga, this super-smart pooch enjoys doing Irish dancing, painting, playing the guitar, helping with the washing and riding a scooter.

KOOLIE
AUSTRALIA

AUSTRALIAN CATTLE DOG
AUSTRALIA

AUSTRALIAN TERRIER
AUSTRALIA

TENTERFIELD TERRIER
AUSTRALIA

CAVOODLE
AUSTRALIA

AUSTRALIAN KELPIE
AUSTRALIA

LABRADOODLE
AUSTRALIA

Australian terriers are said to have a special method for catching snakes – these plucky pooches think nothing of leaping on some of the world's deadliest serpents from behind!

AUSTRALIA and NEW ZEALAND

Until a few centuries ago, the only dogs to set paw in this part of the world were dingoes. But since the arrival of European settlers and their dogs in the late 1700s, the region of Australasia has become somewhere that mixes and matches old breeds and transforms them into totally unique pooches. From early creations like the rugged Australian terrier to much-loved modern crossbreeds like the Labradoodle, these down-to-earth canines are some of the best mates around. Let's say g'day to the dogs from down under.

AUSTRALIAN STUMPY TAIL CATTLE DOG
AUSTRALIA

AUSTRALIAN SILKY TERRIER
AUSTRALIA

An Australian kelpie called Abbie Girl broke the world record for the longest wave surfed by a dog in 2011, when she rode a wave for 107.2 metres (351.7 ft). Go, girl!

NEW ZEALAND HUNTAWAY
NEW ZEALAND

New Zealand huntaways were named after 'huntaway' events at sheepdog trials in the 19th century. During this event, dogs had to drive (or 'hunt') a group of sheep up a hill.

AUSTRALIAN CATTLE DOG

If you're after a laid-back lapdog, turn to another page! The Australian cattle dog is a tough, tireless pooch that likes to be on the go ... ALL the time. But if you can keep up, you couldn't want for a more dependable buddy to zip through the outback with.

The exact origins of this working breed are uncertain, but it has its roots in the 1800s, when British farmers settling in Australia needed a dog that could control the cattle on their vast ranches. They started by crossing an old herding breed called the Smithfield with wild dingoes, then introduced other sheepdogs and kelpies (see opposite) to the mix. Along the way, a branch of this family tree developed into the Australian stumpy tail cattle dog (see opposite). Another became the Australian cattle dog.

Australian cattle dog puppies are born with all-white fur. They develop their blue or red markings a few weeks after birth.

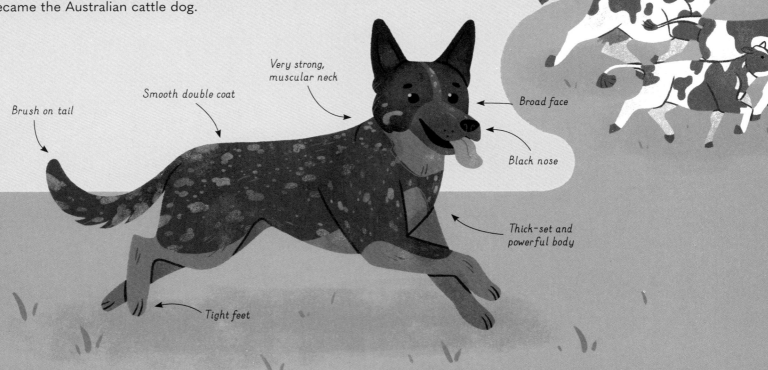

Brush on tail

Smooth double coat

Very strong, muscular neck

Broad face

Black nose

Thick-set and powerful body

Tight feet

POOCH PROFILE:

Country: Australia **Size:** Medium; 43–51 cm (17–20 in) tall **Coat:** Short and smooth; either blue speckled, blue mottled or red speckled **Personality:** Hard-working, agile, intelligent

This smart and speedy breed is also known as the blue heeler or Queensland heeler. These names reflect how the dogs like to work – they nip at the heels of cows to move them in the right direction. Pet cattle dogs will apply this method to anything (or anyone) they feel should be rounded up, so their energy needs to be diverted to tasks like agility or Frisbee sessions to keep them out of trouble.

AUSTRALIAN STUMPY TAIL CATTLE DOG

Although it shares the same origins and always-on-the-go attitude as the Australian cattle dog, the Australian stumpy tail cattle dog (or 'stumpy' for short) is a breed all of its own. Unlike the Australian cattle dog, the stumpy wiggles a distinctive and naturally short tail, which it is thought to have inherited from the Smithfield dog – a British herder that looked a bit like a small Old English sheepdog (p40).

Both the long- and short-tailed dogs were common sights on Australian cattle ranches until the early 20th century, when the popularity of the stumpy-tailed dogs started to decline. By the 1980s, the stumpy was almost extinct. Luckily, it was saved by a breeding scheme set up by the Australian Kennel Club. It's still a rare sight elsewhere in the world, but to Australian farmers this intense, intelligent pooch is one of the best herders in the business.

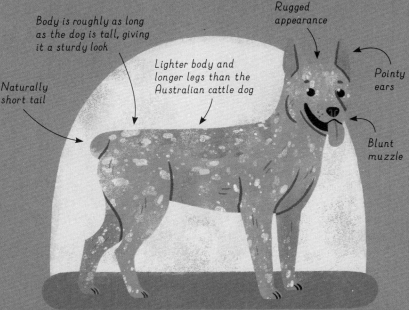

Body is roughly as long as the dog is tall, giving it a sturdy look

Naturally short tail

Lighter body and longer legs than the Australian cattle dog

Rugged appearance

Pointy ears

Blunt muzzle

POOCH PROFILE:
Country: Australia **Size:** Medium; 43–51 cm (17–20 in) tall **Coat:** Short and dense; either blue mottle or blue speckle, or red mottle or red speckle **Personality:** Reliable, hard-working, active

---

These energetic and agile dogs have a signature move of leaping across the backs of sheep to get to the other side of the flock.

Intelligent, keen expression

Fox-like features

Nose colour matches coat colour

Thick neck with a ruff of fur

Tail is slightly curved

Muscly body

AUSTRALIAN KELPIE

Think of the kelpie as Australia's answer to the border collie (p60). Bred from sheepdogs brought from Scotland to the Australian states of New South Wales and Victoria, kelpies were created to guide sheep across huge distances, often working on their own and in very hot, dusty conditions.

Kelpies are as devoted to their human as their work, and love to please and learn new tricks. They can turn their herding skills to pretty much anything that moves – cows, goats and even ducks! – and use their clever brains in a variety of jobs, including search and rescue, detection work and agility. The only problem is, these dogs don't have an off switch. If you share your home with a kelpie, you'll need to remind them to put their paws up at the end of the day.

POOCH PROFILE:
Country: Australia **Size:** Medium; 43–51 cm (17–20 in) tall **Coat:** Short and dense; colours are black, black and tan, red, red and tan, fawn, chocolate, and smoke blue **Personality:** Intelligent, athletic, alert

No one is quite sure where the name 'koolie' comes from, but it's possibly an old slang word for 'collie'.

KOOLIE

Like the Australian cattle dog (p102) and the kelpie (p103), the koolie is descended from sheepdogs that were brought to Australia by British settlers in the early 1800s. The koolie also has a dash of an old German breed, called a tiger dog, running through its veins. Tiger dogs were tough herding dogs, bred to work with flocks in the Bavarian Alps, and they had the same dappled pattern on their coats (called 'merle') as many modern-day koolies.

While the Australian cattle dogs specialised in rounding up cows and the kelpies in herding sheep, koolies worked tirelessly and patiently with both cows and sheep. This flexibility led to different types of koolie popping up in separate regions of Australia – taller dogs for herding cattle in the north and stockier types for keeping sheep under control in the south. Today, koolies are still bred for their talent rather than their looks, so one koolie can appear very different to another.

Tail often has a slight curve at the end

Usually has pricked ears that add to its alert look

Nose and eye colour usually matches coat colour

Lean, athletic body with deep chest

Long, strong legs

POOCH PROFILE:

Country: Australia **Size:** Medium–Large; 46–60 cm (18–24 in) tall **Coat:** Long or short and smooth; colours include solid black, chocolate, red and cream, or merle **Personality:** Hard-working, energetic, intelligent

Pointed ears with rounded tips

Strong neck that carries head proudly

Tail usually sticks up, reflecting the dog's confident character

Compact body

Long, powerful legs

Smooth coat that is easy to care for

POOCH PROFILE:

Country: Australia **Size:** Small; 26–31 cm (10–12 in) tall **Coat:** Short and smooth; white with black, tan or tricolour markings **Personality:** Confident, agile, loyal

TENTERFIELD TERRIER

It looks like a long-legged Jack Russell (p54), but this little dog is an Aussie through and through. The breed is thought to have its roots in rat-catching dogs, such as fox terriers (p42), that were brought to Australia by British settlers in the 19th century. The Tenterfield's ancestors were used to keep ships free from rodents on the long voyage over and later to hunt vermin on Australian farms.

Although Tenterfields have been around a while, it wasn't until 1992 that the breed was recognised by the Australian Kennel Club. This was when the dogs got the name 'Tenterfield', after the Australian town where a well-known breeder lived. These down-to-earth dogs have scampered into Aussie hearts over the years thanks to their adaptability and loyal natures. Today, a Tenterfield is just as happy living with an active family in a city as it is patrolling a farm.

Harsh coat, apart from silky topknot on top of the head

Small, pointed ears

Ruff around neck

Tail carried upright and straight

Strong jaws

Long body

AUSTRALIAN TERRIER

Rounding up cattle and sheep was just one challenge facing Australian farmers in the 19th century. They also needed a hand keeping their homes in the remote outback free from rodents and – scarier still – deadly snakes. The answer was the Australian terrier (or 'Aussie').

This tiny but tough pooch was created on Australian farms in the 1820s by crossing some of the pluckiest terrier breeds, including the Scottish (p44), Cairn, Skye and Dandie Dinmont. Sturdy, smart and primed to pounce on anything that slithered, Australian terriers made splendid pest controllers and watchdogs. At the same time, they proved to be cuddle-bugs when off duty and became much-loved companions. Today, this combination of friendliness and fearlessness makes the Aussie a delightful family pet.

POOCH PROFILE:

Country: Australia **Size:** Small; 25 cm (10 in) tall
Coat: Straight, dense double coat; either dark or light grey with tan, or red **Personality:** Brave, outgoing, eager to please

AUSTRALIAN SILKY TERRIER

Meet the Australian silky – the sleek city cousin of the Australian terrier (above). Sometimes called the 'Sydney silky', the breed was created in Sydney at the start of the 20th century by crossing Australian terriers with Yorkshire terriers (p42). Not quite as small as the Yorkshire but more refined than the rough-and-ready Australian, the silky combines the best features of both breeds.

The silky gets its straight, blue-and-tan hair from the Yorkshire side of the family, and its coat should be brushed several times a week to keep it looking glossy. Although bred to be an elegant household companion rather than a worker, a silky is as smart as it is soft. These spirited dogs can be kept busy with chase games and walks – and they're more than capable of giving possums a fright in the park.

Fine and flat hair, with a silky topknot on top of the head

Small, pointed ears

Long body

Tail carried high when on the move

Hair should be shorter around the feet

Dainty feet and legs

POOCH PROFILE:

Country: Australia **Size:** Small; 23–26 cm (9–10 in) tall **Coat:** Straight and silky; blue and tan **Personality:** Quick, alert, friendly

CUTE CROSSBREEDS AND MARVELLOUS MIXES

Have you ever considered what a combination of your favourites might look like? A 'crossbreed' is a dog whose parents are of two different breeds. Deliberate crosses (also known as 'designer' dogs) have become increasingly popular in recent years. A 'mixed breed' is a dog that is descended from multiple breeds and crossbreeds. Because crosses and mixes can inherit different traits from their parents, you're never quite sure what you're going to get. And that's what makes these dogs extra special.

COCKAPOO

COCKER SPANIEL X POODLE; SMALL TO MEDIUM SIZE

The cuddly cockapoo is one of the earliest 'designer' breeds. First deliberately bred in the 1960s in the USA, these playful pooches combine the jolliness of a cocker spaniel (p18) with the intelligence of a miniature poodle (p49). Another plus is that cockapoos inherit their poodle parent's curly fur, which doesn't shed as much as some other breeds. This can make them a good choice for people who suffer from pet allergies.

PUGGLE

PUG X BEAGLE; SMALL TO MEDIUM SIZE

This adorable cross between a beagle (p46) and a pug (p90) was first developed in the USA in the 1980s and 90s. With the sweetness of the pug and the energy of the beagle, puggles make fun-loving companions. Puggles also tend to have longer noses like beagles. So, while they still keep much of those snuggly pug looks, puggles can suffer from fewer breathing problems than flatter-faced pugs.

POMSKY

POMERANIAN X HUSKY; MEDIUM SIZE

Fallen in love with the husky but don't have enough space? The pomsky might be the dog for you. This feisty fluffball combines the wolfish charm of the Siberian husky (p85) and the liveliness of the Pomeranian (p22) in an adaptable package. Although better suited to city living than a husky, a pomsky is still an energetic dog that needs regular exercise to stay happy. Pomeranians and huskies are both chatty breeds, so this pretty pup will have a lot to say for itself!

LURCHER

SIGHTHOUND CROSS; USUALLY MEDIUM TO LARGE

Lurchers are the result of crossing a sighthound, such as a greyhound (p41) or whippet (p47), with a working breed – normally a collie or a terrier. One lurcher can look very different from one another. Some have shaggy hair, others have smooth fur, and they vary in size. These speedy hounds were bred to hunt small animals such as hares, but, like greyhounds, they have quiet, gentle natures and form very close bonds with their favourite humans. They usually inherit their collie or terrier parent's intelligence, too.

BORADOR

BORDER COLLIE X LABRADOR; MEDIUM TO LARGE SIZE

Mix a pinch of clever collie (p60) with a dash of gentle Labrador (p12) and you get one of the most loving and dependable pooches around. Affectionately known as 'boradors', these dogs are eager to please, devoted to kids and will never, ever tire of a game of fetch. A borador's fur colour often takes after its Labrador parent – either solid black, yellow or brown – with white markings on the chest, paws and tail giving a hint of its collie heritage.

MIXED BREED

A COMBINATION OF MULTIPLE BREEDS; CAN BE ALL SORTS OF SHAPES AND SIZES

From the gorgeously goofy to the splendidly scruffy, you usually can't tell what's gone into making a mixed-breed dog, and that's what makes them so wonderful! Mixed-breeds (also known as 'mutts') are sometimes overlooked because people want a dog that looks a certain way, but these lovable pooches tend to be healthier, longer-lived and easier going than pure-bred dogs because they combine so many different doggie genes. One thing is certain: welcome a mixed-breed dog into your heart and you'll have a friend like no other.

LABRADOODLE

A cross between a Labrador (p12) and a standard or miniature poodle (p49), the Labradoodle was first deliberately bred in the 1970s by the Royal Guide Dog Association of Australia. The idea was to combine the Labrador's kind nature with the poodle's intelligence and low-shedding coat to create a guide dog that would be suitable for people with allergies. The Labradoodle has since become a popular guide and therapy dog, and has lolloped into the hearts of families around the world.

A Labradoodle's temperament and look can vary depending on which parent the pooch takes after. Some may be lively and a little mischievous like a poodle. Others may take after their more easy-going Lab mum or dad. Breeders of Australian Labradoodles sometimes include smaller spaniel breeds in the mix too, which means the size of doodles from down under can range from miniature to large. Whatever their appearance, Labradoodles are enthusiastic, playful dogs that love to be around people – oh, and water!

Square-shaped, athletic body

Big head with a broad muzzle and bushy beard

Long, sturdy tail that is often carried high in a lively manner

Soft, curly coat

Muscular legs

Thick paw pads

POOCH PROFILE:

Country: Australia **Size:** Miniature is 35–43 cm (14–16 in) tall; Medium is 43–53 cm (17–20 in) tall; Large is 53–63 cm (21–24 in) tall **Coat:** Wool-like or fleece-like in texture, with tight or loose curls; colours include black, yellow, chocolate and caramel **Personality:** Affectionate, friendly, smart

Soft expression

Short muzzle

Floppy ears

Coat can vary – either silky like a Cavalier or curly like a poodle

Small but athletic body

Generally, cavoodles don't shed too much.

CAVOODLE

This cuddly canine is the result of crossing a Cavalier King Charles spaniel (p23) with a toy or miniature poodle (p49). Although American breeders may have invented the mix as early as the 1950s, it was first deliberately bred in the 1990s in Australia. Known as the 'cavapoo' or 'cavadoodle' in other countries, it goes by the name of 'cavoodle' in Oz.

Like the Cavalier, a cavoodle is a sensitive soul that loves to snuggle – wherever you go, a cavoodle wants to go too. This makes them affectionate pets, as well as great therapy dogs. They also have a clever, poodle-y side to them that needs to be exercised. Regular walks and games of fetch will do the job, but cavoodles can make great agility dogs due to their quickness and eagerness to please.

POOCH PROFILE:

Country: Australia **Size:** Small–Medium; 22–35 cm (9–14 in) tall **Coat:** Soft wavy or curly fur; colours include black, cream, red, chocolate or a mix of two or more of these colours **Personality:** Sweet, sociable, playful

Collies and huntaways are often used alongside one another on New Zealand sheep farms. The collies round up the sheep while the huntaways follow (noisily!) behind the flock.

Floppy ears

Deep chest

Muscly, athletic body

Long, strong legs

Traditional colour is black and tan

Bred for barking and herding skills rather than looks, so appearance can vary a lot between dogs

NEW ZEALAND HUNTAWAY

You might not have heard of a New Zealand huntaway, but you will certainly hear this dog coming! Huntaways spend most of their day barking at sheep to get them to move, and it's this signature woofing style that makes them stand out from other herding dogs. While a border collie quietly stalks and stares out a flock, a huntaway uses as much noise as possible to get the job done.

New Zealand's only dog breed, the huntaway was developed in the 19th century to work on huge sheep farms, where flocks of around 1,000 sheep were scattered across steep mountainsides. Farmers liked the way their otherwise-silent collies sometimes barked to get the sheep to move – it also meant the farmer could locate the dog if they lost sight of it in the hills. They crossed their collies with heftier breeds, such as Rottweilers (p53) and foxhounds, to create this hard-working, intelligent woofer, with a sturdy build to suit the rugged New Zealand countryside.

POOCH PROFILE:
Country: New Zealand **Size:** Large; 56–66 cm (22–26 in) tall **Coat:** Smooth, long or rough; usually black and tan, sometimes with white or brindle markings **Personality:** Intelligent, friendly, hard-working

GLOSSARY

agility A sport in which a handler guides their dog through an obstacle course in the quickest time possible. Obstacles can include tunnels, jumps and see-saws.

apricot A light to mid-orange colour of fur, and a popular colour for poodles.

assistance dog A dog that has been specially trained to help a disabled person or a person with a medical condition, such as epilepsy.

beard Long hair on a dog's muzzle.

blaze A white stripe that runs up the middle of a dog's face.

bobtail A dog that is naturally born without a tail or with a very short tail.

breed A group of dogs that have been bred by humans to have particular characteristics or features.

brindle A stripy pattern on a dog's coat that usually features two overlapping colours, such as black stripes on a brown base.

canine Any member of the dog (or Canidae) family, including pet dogs, wolves and jackals.

collie Any of several breeds of dog originally used to herd sheep. Breeds referred to as collies include border collies, rough collies and bearded collies.

crossbreed A dog whose parents are two different breeds. For example, a cockapoo is a crossbreed because it is the offspring of a cocker spaniel and a poodle.

dewclaw A claw on the inside of a dog's front leg. Dogs sometimes use their dewclaws to grip things.

Dickin Medal A British medal awarded to an animal that has performed a great act of heroism.

domestication The process of taming a wild animal.

double coat A coat formed of two layers – a rough, weather-resistant topcoat and a soft, thick undercoat.

dryland sledging A sport in which a team of dogs pull a sledge over grass rather than snow and ice.

fawn A soft light-brown colour of fur.

flyball A type of doggie relay race. Teams of dogs have to jump over a set of hurdles to retrieve a ball and bring it back to the starting line in the fastest time.

guide dog A dog that has been specially trained to help a blind person or a person who can't see very well travel around safely. Labradors, golden retrievers and German shepherds make particularly good guide dogs.

heeler Any of several breeds of herding dog that were originally bred to move cattle along by nipping at their heels. Australian cattle dogs and Welsh corgis are examples of heelers.

heelwork to music A sport in which a dog and its handler perform a dance routine set to music.

hound A group of breeds that were originally bred to hunt animals using either smell ('scenthounds') or sight ('sighthounds'). The greyhound and saluki are examples of sighthounds, and the beagle and bloodhound are examples of scenthounds.

kennel club A group of dog breeders that focuses on establishing and maintaining different breeds of dog.

lapdog A small, cuddly companion dog.

litter A group of puppies born to a mother dog at the same time.

liver A brown colour of fur. Also referred to as 'chocolate'.

mask Dark markings around a dog's eyes and on its muzzle.

merle A marbled pattern on a dog's coat, usually made up of darker splodges over a lighter colour.

mixed breed A dog that is descended from multiple breeds and crossbreeds.

mottle A speckled pattern on a dog's coat. Australian cattle dogs have either red or blue mottled coats.

muzzle The nose and mouth of a dog.

paw pad One of the tough, thick patches of skin on the bottom of a dog's feet. The paw pads protect a dog's foot and help with balance.

pepper and salt A coat made up of light grey, dark grey and black hairs. This type of coat is common in schnauzers.

puppy A dog under 12 months of age.

ruff Long, thick hair that grows around the neck.

russet A deep red-brown colour of fur.

search-and-rescue dog A dog that is trained to find missing or injured people.

selective breeding The process in which people deliberately breed animals so they have particular qualities. These can be practical skills, behavioural traits or physical features. The breeds of dog featured in this book are the result of hundreds of years of selective breeding.

sesame A colour of fur created when a dog has a red coat with black tips to some of the hairs.

sheepdog A dog trained to herd and guard sheep.

sheepdog trial A competition in which sheepdogs are tested on their herding skills.

sled dog A type of dog bred to work in teams to pull sledges over snow and ice. The Siberian husky, Alaskan Malamute and chinook are examples of sled dogs.

sniffer dog A dog that is trained to find dangerous items, such as explosives or drugs, using its sense of smell.

spitz A group of breeds that have pointed ears, wedge-shaped heads, thick coats and usually a curled tail that's carried over the back. The Samoyed, shiba inu and Pomeranian are examples of spitz breeds.

tan A light to medium shade of brown.

terrier A group of breeds that were originally bred to chase and catch vermin. 'Terrier' comes from a Latin word meaning 'earth' and refers to the way these dogs would follow their prey underground. The Scottish terrier and wire fox terrier are examples of terrier breeds.

therapy dog A dog that is specially trained to provide comfort to people in hospitals, nursing homes and schools.

topcoat Long, weather-resistant hairs that sit on top of and protect a dog's softer undercoat.

topknot A tuft of long hair that grows from the top of a dog's head.

toy dog A group of small breeds that were originally bred as companions rather than working dogs. The Chihuahua, Maltese and Pekingese are examples of toy breeds.

tricolour A coat of three colours, most often black, brown and white.

undercoat Soft, thick fur that sits underneath a longer and typically rougher topcoat.

whale eye When you can see the whites of a dog's eyes. This usually indicates that a dog is worried or stressed.

wheaten A pale-yellow colour of fur.

wiry Fur that has a harsh texture.

wrinkle A fold of loose skin. A shar pei is an example of a wrinkly breed.

yodel A type of singing that switches between low and high sounds. In the dog world, the word is used to describe the sing-song-like call made by the basenji.

INDEX